# Experience (Still) Matters

## More Essays and Lessons in User Experience Design

Joseph Dickerson

ISBN: 9781703705621

For She Who Must Be Obeyed, my wife Susan. Thanks for your patience as I follow my passions for UX.

## Introduction to new edition –
## "Second verse, same as the first."

Here I go again.

It's been six years since I compiled my essays on user experience design, and since then quite a bit has changed. UX has become more accepted in the enterprise, Design Thinking has become a Big Thing, and how UX and Agile teams work together has been the subject of much conversation. In this time, I kept writing, and speaking, on these and other matters… And thus, this revised edition was born.

I'll keep the net-new thoughts brief, but I wanted to let you know that I kept MOST of the old edition intact, so if you are the 99.988988% of the world who did NOT read that version you will get all the insights contained therein without the dated fatty bits.

Thanks, and I hope you like it.

*Joseph Dickerson, November 2019*

# Introduction to 1st Edition

"Form follows function--that has been misunderstood. Form and function should be one, joined in a spiritual union."

*Frank Lloyd Wright*

"Making the simple complicated is commonplace; making the complicated simple, awesomely simple, that's creativity"

*Charles Mingus*

"It's not enough that we build products that function, that are understandable and usable, we also need to build products that bring joy and excitement, pleasure and fun, and yes, beauty to people's lives."

*Don Norman*

Experience matters.

What does that mean, exactly?

The user experience design discipline (UX for short) is focused on creating solutions that help people live better lives, by serving their needs and letting them do what they want to do quickly and easily... And by providing solutions to problems, some that many users may not even know they have. Well, that's my definition, anyway. Here's Wikipedia's definition:

*User experience design is a subset of the field of experience design that pertains to the creation of the architecture and interaction models that affect user experience of a device or system. The scope of the field is directed at affecting "all aspects of the user's interaction with the product: how it is perceived, learned, and used."*

A rather dry and stuffy definition, this. I like mine better. And it's actually this type of academic "stuffy" definition of UX (that is so often the way it is presented to people outside the discipline) that is a key impetuous behind this book.

I've gone to several UX design conferences in the past and presented at many of them. It's been a while, though, because I've come to realize that most of these conferences tend to be more of a "mutual admiration" society than anything else, with everyone nodding and agreeing to the same thing. The user experience field has matured, and these conferences aren't about convincing anyone on the value of UX - we all "get" that. This maturity means that many conference presentations are less about education and more often about self- congratulation and ego.

IMO this is a long-term threat to the growth of UX design. There is an arrogance shared by many UX designers I've met... Especially with many of the "superstar" speakers at these conferences. It's one thing to know how to do your job, and do it well, it's quite another to think you have all the answers. This attitude is not only unattractive and off-putting, but it lacks in the one thing we UX folks must always have: humility.

I never want to think I know how people think and am always "right". The discovery of how people live, and how we can make their lives better - that is where I always want to be. And that's one of the core things that UX, properly applied, can provide to any company no matter what the domain or the size. And I want more people to understand that.

So, this book is for "everyone else." I want to "evangelicise" UX to people who don't get it - those are the people I want to speak to. This book is for them, a work that (hopefully) explains why Experience Matters, and provides some helpful information and opinions along the way.

This book is not intended to be an instruction manual on how to design, nor is it intended to be a casual read about a domain with little substance. It is a primer on UX design written in a way that (I think) is approachable, conversational and down-to-earth. I want this to be a book for anyone interested in user experience design.

It's not that I don't think some of what I will provide here wouldn't help a fellow designer it can and should, especially if they are new to the discipline. I want to outreach to people who haven't yet "drank the UX Kool- Aid" and explain and promote the domain to them.

Experience Matters is structured into three sections.

The first section, *Tactics*, details processes and methods that can be used to do UX design activities in any organization.

The second section, *Lessons*, discusses things to keep in mind as well as insights I have had over time.

The final section, *Essays*, contains some of my opinion pieces regarding technology, UX design, where the discipline is and where it's headed.

I hope you will enjoy this book as much as I enjoyed writing it. I'm passionate about UX design, and I think that if more companies apply even a modicum of UX to what they create or sell the world will be a better place. It sounds hokey, but I really do believe that if you make something as elegant and as usable as possible then you are making life just a little easier for the consumers of what you have created.

*Joseph Dickerson, January 2012*

# Contents

Experience (Still) Matters

# Lessons

*The following are my thoughts on a broad range of UX topics. Not as practical as the previous section, but I think useful context to understand the UX discipline and things to keep in mind when working on a project.*

# "If we understand the extremes the middle will fall into place."

I just finished watching the great documentary on industrial design Objectified, which has interviews with many of the best designers in the history of the domain, including a personal favorite of mine, Apple's Jonathan Ive.

One moment early in the film struck a chord. The great designer Dam Formosa from Smart Design said that we need to understand the extremes- when designing hedge- clippers, if we understand that many of the people who use such a product are arthritic, and that many others are young and muscular, then supporting both will affectively support the needs of everyone else.

Could we apply such thinking to user experience design? I think so, and I think we already do it when it comes to creating personas.

In order to better understand our users, we create representative personas, based on extensive user interviews, that my team can use to as design "targets." These personas allow me to emphasize with the consumers of my designs so that I can craft solutions that work for them, and not for me (I also try and avoid using the same type of software that I design, to reduce the potential for bias).

The thing that I have found when it comes to personas, though, is something I call the "soft middle" - personas that are accurate but are so similar to the personas in the same range that they are almost indistinct. Whenever me or my team creates such personas, we often label these personas as "secondary" personas, as opposed to the "primary" personas. The ones that represent the extremes.

So, what is the most important things to put into personas? A clear and (preferably) visual representation of the key characteristics and those "extremes". We recently did a mobile research study, to understand how people use their mobile devices - and a key indicator we focused on was the engagement and involvement people had with the mobile technology.

How they thought of the devices, and the usage patterns and mental models we defined, allowed us to better understand what users need to understand to adopt mobile services my company was offering. We learned the extremes, and built personas from them. We could have created nine personas, but found that six primary and one secondary persona represented the data we found in our user research without having a "soft middle."

In summary: define the most important characteristics, target the extremes, and do so by research real users. If you do your due diligence, you'll end up creating solutions that service the needs you find out. Like the man said, solve the problems at both sides of the scale and chances are you'll solve the problems of everyone in the middle as well.

## Content matters.

I've transitioned to a different team on the project I am on right now, away from my current passion around mobile into a more traditional design challenge: product presentment and user engagement. In less pretentious words selling stuff. The group I have joined is as sharp as a razor, and I have very little to add to the conversation - they are on top of things and I am doing my best to not get in the way or break what is already working. I can bring one valuable perspective to the conversation, however, one I'll share here.

Content. It's about the content.

You can design the most elegant engaging and interactive UI ever, but if the information that it contains is muddled or inappropriate or in the wrong tone of voice well, you have created a beautiful silver challis and filled it with cat food (not even GOOD cat food) and then offered the dish to your users.

Sounds appetizing? Of course not. As a communicator first, and a designer second ("to thine own self be true," as the Bard eternally states) I know how important content is. So, for those designers who think that all the world's problems can be solved if we just create a snazzy enough UI as few thoughts.

## Be clear about the point you are making

If you are presenting product information, what is your main thesis? What problem are you trying to solve? What information is you trying to convey? Strip away all the crap, the excess that the stakeholders want you to add. Be pure and true.

## Explain, simply

Why should anyone decide that what you are selling is something you should buy? Tell them, in a way that your 6-year-old can understand. This is not an indictment of the intellectual capacity of the general populace, but a reflection of the increasingly narrow attention spans of the modern adult. We are rushed, distracted - a simple message gets through the noise a lot more than a complicated one. And speaking of your readers

## Know your audience

If you are presenting information in a UI to users who are a lot savvier about technology than the typical Joe, then you can use terms that said typical Joe may not recognize. Simple and clear does not mean generic and homogenized.

## Pay attention to tone of voice

HOW you frame your content is just as important as what you say. I was involved in a project redesigning a Kiosk and that design failed not because the UI did not let the users do what they needed to, but because the tone of voice was too conversational and familiar for the users of the end system. It was jovial, and completely wrong.

Tone of voice is a crucial part of the holistic user experience.

# On loyalty programs, Gamification and good #UX

As anyone who follows me on Twitter knows, I travel for business. A LOT. In the first half of 2018 I traveled internationally twice, and to various cities in the US over a dozen times.

As a frequent business traveler, I have my preferences. And a lot of those preferences are driven not by the experience I get with the service I receive, but instead the perks I get through the various loyalty programs.

Loyalty programs are, at their core, a form of gamification. You get "points" for "playing" the corporations' (program) rules. You can use these points to redeem things – usually free rooms or travel.

But many of the companies providing these loyalty programs are beginning to screw up. Badly. And turning off their customers.

Case in Point #1: Marriott. I used to stay at Marriott all the time, and then they (gradually) started raising the number of points required to get free nights. Eventually you had to stay so many nights to get one free night I decided to stop staying at Marriott.

Here's a good #UX rule of thumb re: loyalty programs – people "absorb" the rules, even if they can't quote a points-to-dollars conversion rate directly. They remember what that is, and when the rules change – well, change is never well received – especially if it impacts YOU.

Imagine you were playing Monopoly, and the rules change mid-game. The player you were playing with (who was also the banker) decides, after building out what he owned, that it now costs a lot more to build houses on Red, Green and Blue properties – the exact same ones you have. THAT is how Marriott (and other companies) make their customers feel when they change their loyalty programs.

Loyal customers feel cheated.

At a certain point, someone at Marriott HQ decided to reduce costs, and increase profits. Fine. That's capitalism. But loyalty programs are about a key feature. LOYALTY. As the old saying goes, it takes a tremendous amount of effort to get a new customer. It takes a lot less to keep an existing one. Loyalty programs should retain loyal customers. Simple, right?

And yet companies like Marriott look at royalty programs as a burden, instead of an opportunity. An opportunity to MAXIMIZE customer spend. By changing the rules, they alienate customers who were loyal to the brand. And lose them to a competitive landscape (Something that IMO the Disney Parks folks are at risk of doing).

Case Study #2: Delta. I booked a trip with Delta a month ago, using SkyMiles. She Who Must Be Obeyed and I were going to Orlando for a weekend. I do not have the status with Delta I used to, I'm now "only" Gold, where at one point in the past five years I was Diamond.

If you are Diamond with Delta, they will bend over backwards to support you. I know this for a fact, because at one point I traveled with a Delta accountant, and he said as much – "If you are Diamond, and you need to be somewhere, they will kick someone off a plane to accommodate you."

Well, I had some business travel that came up that prevented me from taking my personal trip. I had to cancel the trip and discovered that I had to pay Delta a $300 fee to get my 30,000 SkyMiles back. Of course, I had never had to pay such a fee before, because last year I was Platinum. Now, being "only"

Gold, I was less important to @Delta that I was before. Which… when you think about it, is nonsense.

It shows the whole "tiering" system of loyalty programs is ridiculous. I'm "less valuable" as a customer to @Delta now that I'm Gold versus last year, when I was Platinum? Again, inane. I'm still me, whatever arbitrary "tier" a corporation sets for me. Even worse, when I canceled the airfare there was no option on the UI for me to "lose' the points and NOT pay the $300 fee. Because @Delta, clearly, just wanted that cash.

Called Delta customer service to discuss this "new-to-me" fee, and the CSR was pretty much "That's the rules, deal with it." Umm… I'm a close to million-miler customer, and this is the reaction? Another impact of having a one-dimensional loyalty program based (almost solely on) recent spend.

Yes, I know this is all #FirstWorldProblems stuff, and I TOTALLY understand that, but I am #UX designer. Bad experiences rub me the wrong way, and I see how companies are changing things re: loyalty programs and it is so wrong.

As one of my favorite individuals, ever, once stated… "I am not a number. I am a person." Loyalty programs should be centered around the PERSON, not the numbers. And have at least a little bit of memory.

Summing up, if you have a loyalty program, keep in mind that you shouldn't change the rules. If you change the rules, do it to the BENEFIT of the customer, not the detriment. And if you have a long-term customer, keep the whole history of his/her relationship with you in mind… not just the last six months. Next year they may have to travel every week – and they may choose to do that with someone other than you.

# The #UX of Vacations: How technology can provide a better experience

It's summertime, and to many of us that means one thing: vacation. I'm one such person, with two trips scheduled, with a third (potentially) in the offering. Travel of any sort often comes many anxieties... Delayed flights, lost reservations, and long lines at attractions being a few of them. In the past, travel agents used to handle all of the details of trips for you, and while the occupation still exists the 21st Century has brought tools and technology to bear that made the traditional travel agent obsolete.

Kinda.

Because there's still services and values that travel agents provide technology doesn't. The good travel agents provide personal service, getting to KNOW you and your needs in order to steer you towards the right destination and activities once you get there. Yes, you can book your own travel easier and cheaper than through a travel agent, but you have none of the "white glove" treatment that REALLY GOOD travel agents can bring you.

Which is why I have been thinking about how this can change. How intelligent agents and/or a dedicated application can help people plan and have a perfect vacation, as stress-free as possible. What would this entail? Well, here's a few modest ideas.

(And for those travel agents reading this, my intent is not to put you out of work. Mostly.)

### Getting to know you

Good travel agents ask direct questions when they start working with you to plan a vacation. There is no reason an intelligent Bot could not ask the same type of questions. What does your family like? How active do you want to be on holiday? Those type of direct questions can inform a decision tree to not only inform destinations but also planned activities.

And that doesn't stop at simple directional questions. Even better, a smart Vacation Assistant (a term I will be using for the rest of this post) should be able to connect to any and all loyalty programs you have... Providing insights based on your historic travel AND spending habits. Let's say you want to go to the beach – what beach? How far? What type of hotel? Does it need to be near chain restaurants or fine dining? The more your Vacation Assistant knows, the better it can support your vacation planning.

(And yes, this type of machine learning is more than viable with current technology – especially with technology from Microsoft. Trust me, I know…)

## Smart Recommendations (based on what you like and do)

My wife, whom I lovingly call She Who Must Be Obeyed, is somewhat indecisive. Especially when she is faced with an abundance of options to choose from. And that abundance of choice is everywhere – when you have sources like Yelp who lists every place of business within your location, the simple choice of "what do you want for dinner?" Becomes hard for anyone. And when you look at locations like Las Vegas or New York City – home of some of the best restaurants in North America – well, that choice becomes harder still.

Leveraging your travel history, as well as data from your Yelp profile or social media, your Vacation Assistant can let you know what three restaurants near your hotel that fits your tastes and price point.

## A smart itinerary

My wife is not very decisive when it comes to setting an itinerary for activities to do on vacation, so the onus falls on me to do most of that planning.

What would help her (and many others) is a smart itinerary based on the best reviewed most popular activities in the area. This could leverage public data from sites such as Trip Advisor and Yelp as well as social media. It can also be a "bespoke" plan based on what we tell the Vacation Assistant. Again, simple questions can lead to a fully planned set of activities that we can accept or tweak.

## Proactive Notifications

The airlines do a pretty good job letting you know about delays and new gates… but that's not the only thing that people need to know when they travel. What is the UV Index going to be? Is traffic bad at the time of day you are planning to go to a destination? Are there roads closed or construction? And so on.

Leveraging public data and social media, your Vacation Assistant can let you know all this and more, reducing anxiety – or, if the notification is a bad one, at least you'll be in the know.

(You can even build such a solution much like some of the health apps out there do – If the app has access to your fitness device data and see your heart rate is elevated or your sleep is not restful, it could recommend a quick weekend getaway to help relieve some stress. Though being that "smart" of an app may come off as creepy to some.)

## A shareable travelogue

Google Photos does a great job of creating short movies and stylizing images in the background, and that's awesome – but imagine if it also created a true travelogue that showed public images along with your own. Android phones already track where you are (for reasons both good and bad) so why not have an animated map that people can watch highlights along your journey? All of which can be shared though Twitter or Facebook. Again, not hard to do, but a feature that may potentially creep some users out.

## Automatic special requests

If you always stay on a lower floor, or need extra towels, the Vacation Assistant can let the hotel know for you. After setting your preference, the hotel reservations team will get a message letting them know what you like.

There you have it: How an intelligent Vacation Assistant can help take care of your vacation needs, letting you relax… and enjoy your time off.

# How businesses should use social networks

Years ago, I did ethnographic research for AT&T around their stores in order to explore what features should be put in a new point of sale (POS) system. As part of that research I sat in the back of multiple stores in multiple states for weeks, monitoring and documenting every customer interaction. After analyzing the reams of data captured, we found that the stores were not stores at all- they were customer support locations for customers who come in needing help with their handset or their bill. We recommended that they shift their focus on a new POS system to install a better knowledge base and account access tool because of these findings.

Business should look at social as the same thing-it's a customer support channel.

Social is about communicating and (when it comes to businesses) is a place where customers complain about bad service or products. If a company wants to succeed in social, it has to be an active partner with their customers and respond and engage with them in the social space.

You can't just post a profile and let it lie fallow.

You also can't put all your eggs in one basket. As you said, Facebook is the third largest "country" in the world, but Myspace used to be big too. Just like you have to focus your strategy on one mobile channel (of platforms and customers) you have to do the same thing with social. Engage with all the major ones but make one or two your key focus. I think Facebook and Twitter are the two main ones to target.

And how you approach the social network space also depends on the type of business. Take for an example, the domain I am currently design: banking. Banking isn't social - banking is private and personal. Some people flaunt their wealth and status in the social space but not directly - they do it by posting photos of vacations, new possessions, or posting about their experiences. Other industries are better aligned/more "public" and align better with the social media space.

You have to pay attention to what people are saying about your brand in the social space- and how you react to it. You have to be diligent, helpful, and be respectful no matter how the customer "talks" to you. Also, keep in mind the reactionary nature of mobile and the social space - used to be if customers had a problem with a company, they would call customer service, or even write a letter. Now members of the social network respond publicly, and instantly, on their mobile device, often in haste and in anger. You can't respond in kind - you have to maintain your cool and be polite. Because your social response is like e-mail - once it's out there it's OUT there, and can be cross-linked, retweeted, copied. You name it. You have to stay on message, on brand but still have a quick measured response. Don't bicker - it demeans your company and your company's brand.

## How does UX help a company innovate (and/or create "disruptive" innovation)?

User Experience, or User Centered Design, allows you to look at how people work and what they do. The key is to focus on the user needs, to uncover and document opportunities to support people's work flows and therefore define solutions that align with what they actually want to accomplish.

True innovation can only happen if it is informed by this. If you innovate from the outside in (when the technology is the focus) very often companies are defining solutions for imaginary "problems". Take for example the Apple Watch. What problem is it actually solving? You look at the soft sales of the device and you can see that while it has many technology innovations, it's a solution looking for a problem.

On the other hand (literally, in some cases) look at the success of the Fitbit. While it doesn't have half the features and capabilities, it is a product line that is focused on supporting key use cases – mostly around health and activity tracking. By producing a range of products at different price points the company can support different user bases who want to be more active. (The company was so successful that Apple in response "rebranded" the Apple Watch as a fitness device a year after it was released)

Disruptive Innovation happens when companies identify what I consider "key" use cases/user needs and provide a dramatically better experience than the existing status quo. The best example I can think of is Netflix, which supported a key use case (watching movies at home) by first shipping DVDs to customers (which ended up killing the traditional video store such as Blockbuster) and then building a streaming service (which has significantly impacted Cable TV companies' subscriber rates).

## Is User Experience (UX) just where marketing meets development?

The summary answer to your question: no, it's not. Though I can understand why you would get that impression based on the people you have worked with – people who confuse minimalism with user experience design or are calling themselves UX professionals when they clearly aren't.

Just like every profession, there are many levels of professionalism and expertise. I've worked with many "senior" designers who couldn't design their way out of a paper bag, and I've also worked with and mentored junior team members who were absolutely focused on the right things and Could solve any design problem you threw at them. Titles don't matter

– experience, focus, professionalism, humility, and a willingness to learn is key (and I believe that's not just true of UX professionals, but all professions).

UX professionals need to know the domain they are working in but also must bring their own "tools of the trade" to the job – the ability to focus on the user, to identify what they need or want, and to evaluate and design solutions that a company can provide to these users. It's not much more complicated than that, though the tactics and processes we bring to the table are often much more detailed than the essence of what we do.

Feel free to hire and train, but I'd advise you open yourself up and reach out to more user experience designers to get a better sense of both the domain and what they can provide. You may find the right person and hopefully get a better sense of how UX design, applied, can save or make your organization money and help make your customers happy. You may also meet more of the same type of people you have already encountered (as well as some who are unfortunately very pretentious about what they provide) – move past those and get a solid professional.

# How to get hired as a #UX designer (if you've never done it before)

There's a high demand for user experience professionals these days – LinkedIn recently listed UX designer as one of the top 10 hot tech jobs in 2017. If you are interested in the discipline, but don't have any practical experience as a UX designer, you may think you don't have much of a chance of breaking into the profession. Let me correct that pessimistic opinion – while having a degree in design or human factors definitely sets you apart from other candidates, they key to get in the door is to have the skills and the right attitude.

Here's some advice that I hope helps…

## Take advantage of online courses

There are some great courses on UX design that are very inexpensive – my favorites are offered through Lynda.com, and you can start a free trial to check out what courses are available without spending a dime. There you can learn the basics of UX design as well as training on associated areas, such as user research and cloud computing.

## Learn the tools

When it comes to UX design, the more tools you have knowledge of and experience with, the better chances you have at getting a job using them. The core tools are Photoshop, Illustrator, Visio, OmniGraffle, Balsamic, Adobe Experience Design, and Axure RP. The more tools you know (and list on your skills), the better chance you will have at getting past the initial resume review.

The great thing is, almost all of these tools have free trials, so you can play with them before you buy them – and there are also training courses for these tools on Lynda .com.

## Be interested in people

Empathy and an interest in people – how they work, and what they do – is a key skill that any designer who creates interfaces that users engage with needs to have. Being interested in what users need to know and accomplish allows you to create more effective experiences.

It will also allow you to ask the right questions of potential or existing users to ensure you are able to illicit user requirements to inform your designs.

## Use the latest technology

Being adept at technology allows you to be better at designing solutions that leverages newer technology. So, get (or try out) the newest apps and devices, within reason (and budget). Upgrade your computer, tablet and phone. Get accustomed to the "design language" that all these devices reflect and use.

## Have a modern design portfolio (and put it online)

Even if you have not been paid to design anything, that doesn't mean you can't create a portfolio. Identify a "problem space" or industry you are interested in, define a use case, and design something.

It may take some time, it may take some iterations, but you can build a good portfolio with a little effort. Ask your friends and family give you feedback as you are working to make sure you do your best (and elicit real feedback, not hollow "it looks great" quotes).

You want to show you can do the work before you get the job... and once you have something good put it online. Use free hosting services like WordPress to upload your work and use URL shortening sites like Tiny URL to create a personalized link.

## Have (and show) attention to detail

When you build your portfolio, make sure you show a lot of detail in your wireframes or design documents. The reason why is simple: the more details you display in this work, the more confidence hiring managers will have in your ability to do your job effectively. Developers need detailed design specifications to build applications and sites, and if you show you can provide this type of documentation it will increase your chances of getting a position.

## Don't be arrogant

Finally, don't be cocky. You need to be confident in the natural or learned skills you have, but also need to work well with others and collaborate. Being (or coming off as) arrogant does you no favors, either when you are trying to win the new job or after you land a design position.

The world of UX design changes every day, because people change every day. Being a good designer means you need to constantly refresh your skills and understanding of users and being an arrogant "know it all" will always get in the way of that. Always.

## Resistance: What stops users from doing things new or different?

In my career as a user experience designer and researcher, I've interviewed or tested scores of end users through the years, and I see a trend show up over and over. Users have often told me that they KNOW that how they "do" something is not the "right way" or that they were aware of a new feature or method that was available to them, but they never change or adopt the new offering. This was never tied to a particular demographic or class of user but was a consistent pattern of behavior that I observed no matter what the product or topic being studied.

So, what is the root cause of such behavior. Obviously, I'm not a mind reader, and at first I thought this topic was something that was worth further study (maybe even worth of writing a book on it) and I may look into this further (especially as part of my job will soon involve figuring out how to get past the mental barriers I am discussing here).

My interest in this is piqued even more by the observation that trying something new or different in a piece of software is just the tip of the iceberg - people stop themselves from trying new things, taking risks, etc. throughout their lives. For a good analysis of this type of behavior in the creative area, I recommend The War of Art, a fine book by Steven Pressfield.

So, though I may never have "enough" to write that book on this topic, I have gathered some observations that I think explains some of the behaviors I've noted. I use the general term "resistance" here - Resistance to change, resistance to new features, resistance to moving tasks from one "place" to another, etc. Here's some causational factors:

### Fear of change

Change is scary to lots of people, and when we introduce a completely revised UI that varies greatly from the interaction models, they expect to see we often get a fear response from the participants we are surveying. It's not that they would not be interested in the new design, it's just the immediate response is negative because it's "different."

## Habit

If I had to guess, I would say that we are all creatures of habit to some extent- some more than others. I have seen many instances where users, shown a different way to do a task (one that they themselves acknowledge is better than the way they accomplish the task currently) are resistance to the new method. "It's the way I've always done things." These participants, when interviewed, say they will "give it a try" when the new design is implemented. Don't count on it.

## Apathy

This is closely aligned to the habitual behavior, detailed above, but this is when the user just doesn't have enough emotional energy invested in the task to change how he or she goes about doing it. This is usually when the task is a "rote" one, which varies little from day to day (or month to month). Getting past such apathy is a daunting challenge.

## Ignorance

Many times, I have exposed users to functionality that they can already DO in their existing systems, and they express surprise at the capability. A great example of this, outside my own designs, is when Microsoft redesigned the UI for their Office suite.

One of the most requested features- the ability to watermark a document - had been there the entire time, but the redesign placed the control in a more prominent place based on the context of what the user was attempting to do. It quickly became the most frequently used function in Office.

In this case, the user is not resisting the option-they know there should be a way to do the task, they just don't know how. The design has failed the user, and unnecessary frustration often occurs.

## Overload

Many UIs (including a few that I have had a hand in designing) are really, well, too much. I had the opportunity to design an interactive voice response system at Cingular Wireless, and what I quickly discovered was that cognitive overload was a Clear and Present Danger when it comes to creating such a system- users quickly got overwhelmed if you provided too many prompts, especially if the prompts did not match the "mental model" of what they were expecting or trying to do.

The same lesson applies to UI design- if the UI you provide users is too cluttered or has distracting elements, you will see many "give up" because it's "too much" - to these users, the cluttered design makes figuring things out WORK - and you have lost them.

How do we "get past" these barriers as UI and user experience designers? Well, first off, we need to remind ourselves that we only design part of the experience - the stuff that, usually, is on a screen that people interact with. The user's mental models on how things should work, the physical environment -

all of that STUFF - we can't control. Most of the time we can't even influence the hardware that users pull on, push and tug on to access/use our designs. So, we need to accept that there is going to be some natural "resistance" to anything we offer, because of these factors outside our control.

What is important to do is understand when such resistance may occur and keep the above causes in mind. It will help us make a more focused design that will increase adoption of the systems we design and make our end users (and our bosses) happier.

## How to get a 360-degree view of your users

I'm a passionate advocate of user research, not just as a practical matter but also from a strategic viewpoint – The more you know about the people that engage with the solution or product you produce the better you can model and "tune" that offering to support those users. Optimally, you start from the users (potential or actual) and then you build the offering based on what you know about them – though most organizations aren't that user-centered.

I had a great chat recently with my team members about the difference between Lean and Agile UX – to me, Lean is the above strategic view of user needs (to inform product features and road-maps) and Agile UX involves the tactical activity that involves designing the detailed experience and iterating on those details using user feedback. In the end, the core of both is what UX is all about – know the user, solve for the user, and help the user. The only real difference is your area of focus.

Today, let's cover the phase gates that I think are

required to gather a comprehensive "360-degree view" of users, to inform the strategic product road-maps for new and future products.

## Identify who your users are

Sounds simple, but this is actually a pretty important activity. If you don't have a correct "target" for your research, you will spend time gathering data and doing analysis on people who may never use your product. A good example was when I was doing small business research a decade ago. What type of small business? What size? How old has it been in operation? Family-founded or franchise? Know the answer to those questions, informed by marketing research and telemetry data, allowed us to focus on the 80% "core" audience who used or would be interested in the products the company was taking to market.

## Walk a mile in their shoes

Having a hour-long interview is one thing – parking yourself in the user's workspace while he or she go through their daily routine is something else entirely. I'm a true believer in observational ethnography, and I have seen first-hand the insights that can come from doing this activity. Get as many opportunities as possible to "walk the walk" and shadow users for a full day.

Don't interrupt, take notes, and ask questions when and where is appropriate. People will often do things in their routine unconsciously, and if you pay attention and ask later, "Why did you do that?" You'll pick up some keen insights and understanding.

### Interview with "two ears, one mouth"

One of the best pieces of advice came to me when I first started Microsoft six years ago, which is "Two ears, one mouth". You should spend twice as much time listening as you do talking. And REALLY listen: Be "present" and engaged in the conversation. As so many people are distracted and casual conversations are usually exactly that – casual – you will be surprised at the response of the interview subject if you practice this "active listening" approach.

### Use all the data you can

If you think your organization doesn't have useful legacy data you can use to understand your users, you are almost certainly wrong. Even companies with limited analytics and marketing research have data that can inform your understanding and insights. Just be mindful to keep the context and age of this data in mind – user expectations and behavior patterns change all the time, and data that is six years old is a lot less relevant and useful compared to data that is "just-in-time" information.

### Consider multiple approaches and teams (if you can afford it)

I've never been a fan of heavy-handed research. I think a smart lean (pun unintended) team can be more efficient and gather as many insights as a larger group. It's also easier to manage and coordinate. Try and get as many views of the users by doing more than one technique – observation, interviews, focus groups, design thinking workshops, service design blueprinting, what have you.

### Be aware of "Compassion Fatigue"

A growing sentiment in UX research is regarding the impact that research has on the researcher – especially when the topic of inquiry involves people who are going through rough times. A research partner of mine almost a decade ago was doing research into how the lower and lower-middle class manage their money – and it nearly broke my heart. Be mindful of the mental health of the research team to make sure they are not burning out – and also that their sympathy towards the research subject's situation is not biasing their analysis and insights.

### Spend enough analysis time

Research is 50% fact gathering, 50% synthesis and analysis. If you don't have such a balance, you will not be able to mine that rich vein of data for all the insights it provides. You have to "do the work" and that means different passes at the data, reviews and collaboration, and final findings definition.

### Be ready to do it all over again

Users perceptions, habits and work flows change over time. You have to take a "longitudinal" view on research, and accept that perfect is the enemy of good. You have to stop one phase of research, to deliver actionable insights, and at the same time (if you have sufficient executive support) you need to be planning the next round of research. When I was doing small business research, we revisited the topic months after the first go round... And identified that the world had (if only slightly) changed. Be aware of the shifting baseline, and always keep learning.

# Tactics

*The following are "how-to" guides on specific UX topics. Dive in, and I hope you can use some of these ideas to either start doing UX design or refine how you work.*

## What are some good ways to start learning user experience design?

First, understand that the user experience design is applied across multiple industries and areas - software, service design, retail, hardware, you name it.

You should focus on the domain that you want to work in and learn as much as you can in that domain. If it's hardware, spend time understanding industrial design and production methods used to ship physical products. If it's retail, learn the rules around merchandising and crowd patterns. And so on.

Then, learn and read about some tactics and best practices in user experience design. Learn how to do user research and ethnography, create personas, do usability testing, document designs, create prototypes, etc. Most of these practices can be applied across multiple domains, and you can apply them whatever you "land" in your career. This book is a good start and covers some of the high-level aspects of these areas.

Next, focus on your listening skills and empathy. The more you listen the more you understand the needs of end-users and empathy allows you to design solutions to solve their problems, and not just designs that "look good."

Find a mentor and have them walk you through a previous design project. Pull out all the design artifacts, from concept design to detailed specifications. View videos from any usability tests that took place.

Understand the process that was followed to go from a high-level problem statement and concept(s) to a detailed and final solution. And don't try and do this all at once... Take the time to understand things thoroughly.

Finally, do the work. Don't wait for an opportunity to do UX design, just start doing it. Define a small project to work on and leverage the same methodology you just detailed. Accept that you are going to be wrong and then get more "right" as you iterate and learn.

# What are the benefits of user experience design?

There are several benefits to user experience design, and I'll list some of them. Before I begin, a quick note: user experience design to me encompasses EVERYTHING, from UI design to customer support processes to retail store design and packaging. So, when I speak of "user experience" I'm thinking about any touch point a user can have with a company.

### Increased customer satisfaction

The better experience you create for your customers, the happier they will. And the opposite is also true: the worse experience you provide to your customers they will become more and more frustrated with what you are providing them...

And they will be far less likely to recommend your offering to friends and families. And dissatisfied customers call to complain, which means when you provide a good experience you also have...

**Reduced cost of ownership and support**

If you produce a product (hardware or software) that has an easy-to-learn (and easy-to-use) design, you will have to support that product less. Good design also reduces your total "cost of ownership", in that you will need less documentation, a smaller support staff, and less salespeople. Which brings us to...

**Increased sales**

Happy users share their happiness with their circle of friends and family. They also review your offering online. Providing a good experience helps build positive word of mouth and increases sales. It also often results in increased customer loyalty and therefore repeat business.

**Good karma**

OK, this one is not really a measurable benefit, but I think that if you create something that helps people do something well and makes their lives better then you will benefit from that effort. Case in point: One of my first major successes in user experience design was the creation of a streamlined process to sign up for electronic bills. This process resulted in a huge "hockey stick" uplift in adoption, which in turn meant a lot less trees were destroyed to print paper bills. My company did well, it had a positive environmental impact, and the success helped my career. Win, win, and win.

## How do you teach someone user experience design?

I will caveat my guidance in this area by stating that there are "soft skills" that all good user experience designers have: problem solving, empathy, communication skills, and collaboration. If a person starts out with a deficiency in one or more of these areas, they will not only have a more difficult time in the UX profession, but it is a real possibility that they are not suited to work in the domain in the first place. That being said...

How to teach user experience design? By combining the practical with the academic and throw in a huge dash of DOING.

The foundational stuff - basic logic, psychology, design principles, art appreciation, software design processes - that is your "introductory" class - UX 101. Make sure that foundation is firm as you can make it.

The next class, UX 201... That's where you introduce real- world design problems. In this class, I'd start by designing a "brand new" offering, and then after we cover all the bases, I'd have the students focus on redesigning a product... Which takes a different approach than a "green field" design process.

Start with detailing how to do user research to inform your understanding of a domain. Walk through analysis techniques that can be used to form concepts, personas and mental models from the user research data. Look at the different ways software development life cycles can - or can't - align with a user-centered design process. Then I'd teach techniques in design testing, design prototyping, and design documentation... The practical real-world skills that takes concepts to reality. All this would be as hands-on and collaborative as possible.

Finally, in UX 301, I'd cover various case studies in UX design, and also review communication techniques and skills that effective designers need to use to get their design "across the line" with decision makers and business stakeholders... A vital skill that is under-taught and under appreciated.

## What are some good ways to plan a UX project?

The first thing is, what kind of project is it? A research project? A new product? A revamp of an existing offering? Testing of an existing project? The techniques and the team you need to apply and gather will vary greatly depending on what the project is.

That is the foundational stuff. When it comes to the project itself, you need to staff the right talent to support the goals. If it's a site revamp and a revenue play, you'll need a graphic designer and an interaction designer as well as a design lead (who optimally should be the person who did the aforementioned customer interviews). Define the steps that need to occur and the amount of rigor that is required based on budget and timelines. Do you need two rounds of usability testing or one? Do you need to have multiple checkpoints with stakeholders, or just a final readout at the end of the project?

Don't be dogmatic about your plan - be prepared to be flexible and understand that life is about compromise. You will have deadlines, and you will (in all probability) not be able to do all the research or design activities that you want to do.

# How (not) to manage a UX project

I've worked on a lot of different projects in my career, and I've learned quite a bit. I've always said that I'd rather learn from someone else's mistakes instead of my own, but I've had ample opportunity to learn from my own missteps too.

I see a lot of UX articles that detail how to successfully execute a design project, but I haven't seen much discussion on things or steps to avoid. So, based on mistakes I've encountered along the way (some mine, and some observed), as well as conversations I have had with some peers, here are some ideas on how not to manage a design project.

Note: Just to be clear, the following details things you SHOULD NOT do if you want a successful project. Trust me, I learned the hard way. Names have been changed to protect the innocent (and my ass).

## Go straight to detailed design

"Just do wireframes," is what the project manager told my team and me on a high-profile effort, because that is all that we had a "contractual obligation" to provide. No analysis phase, no user research, no design iterations — just go straight to detailed design.

Well, that didn't work, because… we went straight to detailed design. We didn't have a shared "vision" for the design team to follow … and we weren't allowed to invest the time to create one. A high-level design wasn't something we "had" to deliver, and the project went badly.

## Treat Use Cases as unquestionable laws

I like use cases, I really do. I used to write lots of them. But when the use case explicitly directs the design direction (because the business analysts think it's their "job" to do that) and the management team says, "design what's in the use case" … well, you're setting yourself up for conflict and potential failure.

Why? Because use cases are usually focused more on business rules and logic and less on what the optimal experience should be for users. You need both, and blind adherence to use cases may result in the creation of a solution that may not align with what users want and need. And while business analysts are usually very bright and intelligent people – most of them aren't user experience professionals.

## Skip user testing

This one is obviously a bad idea, but I've been surprised at how often the need for user testing has to be argued for, even in "savvy" user-centered organizations. Often user testing is cut because of budgetary constraints, or stakeholders say, "why should we test, the design team knows what they are doing." As good as your team is, design testing is far cheaper than designing in a bubble and then investing huge amount of money and time deploying an untested direction.

## Don't create a "High-Level" design

As stated above, you must have a direction that all the designers can align to and follow. It can be a set of best practices, a declaration of principles, a conceptual model of usage … But SOMETHING has to exist to ensure consistent and successful work. Want your project to fail? Then don't bother to do all this drudgery and work.

## Use an inflexible design process

I once worked with a project manager who was a "checklist" guy. Now, I love checklists, but if you follow your process/checklist blindly without any flexibility you are going to end up in situation where quality is not the focus, crossing things off a list is. You have to be flexible and be willing to change plans as needed, based on revised requirements, test results, or what-have-you.

Unless you want to fail, of course.

## Prevent designers from collaborating

If you really want to fail, put designers on separate features and don't let them talk to one another. One major project started out doing exactly that, and the designers were also under tight deadlines. The result was a Frankenstein's Monster of a design that was inconsistent and impossible to implement. Though, if this is your goal, congratulations! You did it!

## Hire arrogant designers

We all have various degrees of confidence in our abilities —we gain this confidence over time as we gain more experience doing what we do.

There's confidence, and then there's arrogance … and if you want to fail, hire arrogant designers who think they know it all. You will quickly discover that these people alienate their colleagues and stakeholders and produce work that isn't nearly as good as they think it is.

## Skirt accountability

If you are on a design project that is use-case driven, and the use-case is "the law of the land," it's really tempting to just do what the use case says; to put in your eight- hours and go home. That's the wrong way to approach design. The right way is to challenge the assumptions that are in the use cases and produce designs that aren't "by the book." Don't give up, man up.

### Never ask, "Who's in charge around here?"

One of the first things I ask for is a RASI chart, a list of who is in charge and who the key stakeholders are. That way I will know whose opinions to heed and whose I can (safely) ignore. If you don't have those roles clearly defined, then everyone's opinion will "count" and it will turn into a painful design-by-committee situation.

### Have a super-critical stakeholder with bad communication skills

If you want a design project to fail, then find the most critical person in your organization and make him or her the person who reviews and approves all the designs.

Not only will he or she be negative but, because they have poor communication skills, they won't tell you why they don't like it. The result will be demoralized designers (and a revolving door they quickly leave through).

### Have meetings without agendas and expected outcomes

This is an obvious one and is not just how not to do a design project, it's how not to do any project. The larger the organization is, the more frequently useless meetings seem to pop into everyone's calendar. A meeting without a purpose is a waste of time and money that can be better spent creating good designs

## Conclusion

There you have it, eleven ways you can ensure your design project ends badly. Or, you can avoid experiencing such a dire predicament by doing the opposite - and making sure that the project applies a thorough user-centered focus and methodical process.

# What UX design process should I follow?

I've written up and followed about a half-dozen UX design processes over the past dozen years, and the more projects I work on the more I realize that process is only as good as the inputs you have, the talent on your team, and the time you dedicate to design. UX design is knowledge work, and there is no "optimal" process that guarantees results.

(In my mind, I can hear some of my colleagues reading this and going "WRONG!" and flinging this book across the room in response to the above, and that's fine. We'll agree to disagree.)

The way I look at it, is there's some core steps that need to be followed in ALL UX design projects, and the amount of rigor and time that you apply to these core steps depend on the timeline and budget you have. Here's those foundational steps:

**Know your users and their needs**

DUH. It's a no-brainer, but sometimes the obvious is not- so-obvious. You need know the target audience for what you are designing and what they need/want/desire.

Shakespeare wrote "the readiness is all" and before you are ready to dive into UI design you have to understand those two core things. I have seen WAY too many projects end badly because the design team jumped into UI design early without doing this foundational thing.

There are best practices that can be borrowed and applied from other industries to do this, and I've borrowed two key processes from journalism and film pre-production to define my "foundation."

The first is the Journalism 101 principle of Who What When Where and Why:

Who is this design for? Find out is who the client's customers are. Are they middle-class housewives? Gen Y hipsters? If you don't have an understanding of who the customers are then you will have a hard time designing a solution for them.

What will they be doing? What are the core tasks that the design needs to support?

When will they use it (how often)? Once a day? All day long? This impacts how "learnable" you need to make the design.

Where will they use it? What is the context of use? Is this a "modal" app for a mobile phone or is it an application that is accessed along with three or four other discrete systems?

Why would they use it (as opposed to another process or application)? Is it by choice, or is it a tool that management makes staff use?

This last question gets to the heart of the value proposition of what is being designed/developed. In my opinion, if you can answer all these questions to YOUR satisfaction, then you are ready to get to the next step in the design process.

So, how do you get the answers? Well, some of these answers can be provided by the business analysts you are working with, or the key stakeholders But I've found that the best way to get the answers is to talk to the users themselves, to understand their workflows, their needs and frustrations by doing it yourself the answers will be more "personal" to you and will remain "top of mind" as you do your design work.

## Define candidate solutions

Once you know the users, define candidate solutions. These can be anything - sketches, stories, or a set of features. Brainstorm ideas. Create conceptual models and artifacts.

**Tell the story**

The second key process is documentation of the above. Tell the story of the users and the proposed solution(s), either through storyboards or user stories. I don't think you need both, as they both service the same need. You should do whatever you are most comfortable doing... If you're a person who sketches a lot, do storyboards. If you enjoy writing, then do user stories.

The point of this is to define a "flow" of the tasks that the users do in and with what you are designing - always keep in mind this is NOT UI design, you are capturing and defining the user experience. You can share these artifacts with key stakeholders to review and get consensus and THEN, after all are agreed, start doing the interface design work.

Part of this step involves documenting the users as well - this is often done by using/creating personas, which are "characters" that I usually create based on such interviews and ethnographic research, but you may not have that luxury or opportunity. Personas give you an empathetic target that you can use in design activities and are very effective.

**Get user feedback**

Flesh out the designs into something that you can step users through. The fidelity of this effort should be low, because it's "early days" yet. Sketches are fine, as long as they are clean and obvious enough for someone with no previous understanding of the design to understand. Walk them through the design and have them explain the designs to YOU. This is the best kind of feedback to receive.

### Refine, redesign, and test

Take the user feedback and refine the designs. Flesh out areas of the experience that require additional detail. Create a more detailed accessible version of the designs and/or create a prototype the users can actually use. Test this prototype with users.

### Detailed documentation

Document the design in whatever medium that is preferred. Define how the design works - what happens when controls are clicked, when pages load. Also define what happens when the user makes mistakes, and make sure that they can recover from such mistakes gracefully. If you have the ability to do so, you should also document the overarching UX Architecture that you have defined.

These are the foundational process steps - your process (and mileage), may vary, but I think you'll find most of these core activities are the ones that you return to again and again. More details about some of these steps are contained in the following section.

# What is a High-Level Design?

I've been in several meetings where the words "high level design" was bandied about by designers and stakeholders. The importance of a high-level design... well, it was unquestioned. A high-level design was absolutely vital, to ensure the success of the project.

Everyone agreed needed one, of course.

At one such meeting, a long time ago, someone asked the obvious question, "What is a high-level design?" That person was me. I kinda sorta knew what it was, but not really. My asking resulted in a very heated discussion with my fellow designers. I found out that none of the people in the room could define it succinctly... and several disagreed with each other's definitions. We hashed it out and settled on a definition that was agreeable to all concerned.

After some research, I've settled on my own personal definition of what a high-level design is, and what it brings to a design project – which is quite a lot, in my opinion.

A high-level design represents the "foundation" of what you are trying to produce as a design solution. It is the core definition of what it is, who it's for, why you are doing it, and what it will do. It contains details about user needs, business drivers, design principles, the core conceptual model of how people do things, and the core interactive model that the design needs to follow. A potentially more approachable way to think about it is to look at it as a brief such as one that would be given to an ad agency, a "project charter" for a UX team. So, now, the big question: how do you create one, and how do you use it? The following sections outline what I have done on a couple of projects to create a high-level design.

### First, know what you know

Even if you haven't formally done any research in the domain you are designing, you probably already know a lot about the space. Get it down. Do you have access to any research about what you are doing? Study it and capture the key learnings that can apply to this project. Have different people look at the same data, to get a different perspective. Throw all this stuff up on the walls where you are working and do an affinity exercise to organize it and identify trends and patterns.

### Talk to business stakeholders

Get a sense of what is important to them on the project and capture what they know. Depending on the experience of the people involved, they may be able to provide volumes of contextual information and understanding. An added bonus: you can capture, and keep in mind, the business goals of the project, to sanity check the design work against.

### Define who you are designing for

Use or create personas to have an empathetic "target" for your work. Capture and/or define the "I want to" users bring to what you are creating. Understand the emotional and rational landscape that exists in the space, so you can either align with the desires ("I want to be noticed") or identify potential points of resistance ("I don't want to spend a lot of time doing X").

### Create a conceptual model

Visualize the space in a way that represents what people do in the domain you are presenting, based on all of the above "intelligence" you have gathered. Keep it simple and approachable and consider using visual weighting to represent aspects of the experience that is more important than others.

A quick case study: My team created a model for mobile banking that represented what people did in a mobile banking context. We identified five areas of action, and also noticed that, frequently, one action could lead to another.

The visual we did presented the inter-connective aspect of the domain and highlighted the key actions.

It was very helpful as a reference doc that we could then "map" features to, and therefore prioritize them.

## Sketch and collaborate

Take all the above and start sketching out how it could work. Use key functions as the basis of what you are sketching. "Sketchstorm" together, to compare and share ideas. Through elimination and discussion, identify some key sketches and ideas that look best. Flesh these out in something that you can get feedback on.

## Test and refine

Get the conceptual sketches out to users. See if they can understand how the intended UI would work. Have the participants describe to you how it would work, to see if it is obvious enough and quickly understandable. Refine the design based on testing.

## Create a draft information architecture

Group the functions and the information, using the aforementioned conceptual model to group like things and to make the more frequently accessed "stuff" be front and center, and the less important "stuff" at a lower level. Document the final IA when the design is done.

## Define the interaction model

This is more for a mobile or table app than a web app, but you need to define how users engage with the information and functionality. Is it pinch? Swipe?

Using pagination?

## Document and package

It can be contained in one page or a hundred pages, but the more concise you make it, the better. Present it to stakeholders to get buying and (if needed) approval. Keep all your working artifacts if you need to use them to "show your work" to any skeptics.

Doing a high-level design is absolutely crucial to ensure success. It allows everyone to create and share a core vision as to what they are doing, a vision that the design team can then follow through on and quickly execute.

Try it, it works.

## Some thoughts on design tools

What design tool should you use to do UX and UI design? Whatever tool works best for you.

I've used A LOT of design tools in my life and looking on the list of tools out there I dare say I've tried a majority of them. After many months of use, I can tell you what works for me... Usually. That would be either OmniGraffle or Axure, but paper pencil and whiteboards also are more than sufficient.

Here's the thing, and the main point I stated above - there is no "best" tool for designing mobile apps, just as there is no "best" tool for designing desktop or web apps. The tool that designers use are the ones they have, use and are comfortable with... Not one that will make the ideas "happen" automagically.

Design is work, work requires tools, and a poor work blames his tools (as the saying goes). Create a great app and focus on the problem you are trying to solve, not the tools you are using. Tools won't make a bad design any better.

## Peer designing

There's a practice in software development called peer programming, where two developers' partner with each other to code a particular project. It allows for each developer to play to his or her strengths and to "cross- train" with a colleague. In the projects I've worked in that applied such an approach I've seen this work quite well and a conversation I had with a colleague last week made me realize that the same practice would add value to user experience design.

This realization was a long time coming, and one that comes as I have reached a certain maturity in my profession and my abilities. When I was younger, I thought I was a Superman, that I needed no help, that I could solve all design problems by myself. Time has shown me the error in such an approach, and some of my best work has come in partnership with other designers. In fact, I've begun to realize that success in any creative endeavor needs open collaboration an artist needs critics and partners to make the good work better.

Here's the aspects of peer designing that are note-worthy (in addition to the points stated above):

### Collaboration.

The obvious point, and the one typified by the cliché "Two heads are better than one." Collaborating on a design problem or in a design space allows for two (potentially dramatically) different approaches to be discussed and defined. You have someone who responds to you and vice versa.

### "Explain your design."

By having a design partner, you have to continuously explain the design rationale behind the decisions you have made, which provides useful "practice" when the time comes that these designs need to be presented to stakeholders.

You are not alone.

Designing in isolation is sometimes a very lonely situation and having another person in the thick of things provides an unmeasurable amount of comfort, especially if there is a tight deadline. It helps.

### An opportunity for mentorship.

Peering senior design professionals with junior designers allows for an excellent opportunity for mentorship and cross-training. I note the latter because, unlike old dogs, senior designers should still be open to new ideas and techniques from (often younger) junior designers.

So, if you are working on a UX design project or planning one, think about structuring your team in pairs. It has many notable aspects, and it may result in a superior design solution. It has when I did it.

## User research and participatory design

I've done a lot of user research - from quick prescreening interviews to full blown ethnography - and no matter what the scope of what I'm doing is, I always get some nugget of insight each time I talk to the (eventual) consumers of my designs.

Such insights can be very slight and may only reinforce a finding from previous project- and then some force you to change your entire design approach.

Because of this consistent and incredibly useful benefit, I often tell my peers that I could not do my job without such research (which often feels more like casual conversations than user study). If, someday, my budget was cut and my research was no longer funded, I'd still do it - only I would be accosting random people at a local mall.

Recently its gone past the insight and study stage-

I've started to take advantage of the times I have with users to basically "codesign" with them. Some of my colleagues find fault with this approach (they tend to be more dogmatic about things) and my response to their criticism is a simple and direct one - they are the user, shouldn't you let them give a say in the product you are going to foist upon them?

"Users aren't designers," is the usual response, and I can't disagree with that. But I'm looking for inputs, feedback, and understanding of what works for the people I am interviewing; why shouldn't I take their design ideas with as much weight as those of one of my product stakeholders?

So, the long and the short of this? If you are a user researcher don't be dogmatic, open yourself up to doing participatory design along with your research - you may find your users have some pretty interesting design ideas you had never thought of.

## Empathy encourages better design

One "trick" I have noticed in many movies is the writer has something "bad" happen to the main character very early in the film. This is intended to provoke a sympathetic response from the audience - and, optimally, an empathetic one. Because, if the audience empathizes with a character, then the viewer becomes more engaged and involved in the "hero's journey" - they share the aspirations and goals of the lead and when the hero "wins", the audience does as well.

I content that there are two masterful examples of this in two of my favorite films. The first is in the original Star Wars, and it's when Luke Skywalker is told by his aunt and uncle he cannot leave and follow his dreams at the Academy - Luke is facing the same obstacle so many of us have had, which is the day-to-day responsibilities of life. He wants to leave, he can't leave. and we empathize. We all have some hopes for a better life in some way, and we feel for Luke. He is Us, and when he "escapes" his responsibilities he is able to become the hero he dreamed of being. and so are we.

The second masterstroke in this regard is the recent (and wonderful) Pixar movie UP. We see Carl Fredericksen live almost his entire life in a 10-minute sequence that shows how his and his wife Ellie's hopes and dreams were defeated by the day-to-day aspects of life (the car's tires need replacing, the roof is destroyed in a storm, they are unable to have children). And then

SPOILER!

Ellie dies. Whatever happens for the rest of that movie, you CARE about Carl, even though he looks like an Easter Island head in profile. THAT is fantastic writing.

So, how does this apply to user experience design, the art of making products and systems that service the needs of users far and wide? The same way that empathy matters to these movies, it should matter when we create these designs for our customers. Empathy can come from the applied use of personas, created from user research.

Personas detail all the aspects that matter when it comes to the users of your systems. They are, to a very large extent, your characters.

When you CARE about your users (as represented by personas) you focus more, and spend more time putting yourself "in the place" of your users. And this is not just something that the UX professionals should do. Personas should be promoted throughout the development and product organization, and when it is, I have found that the same empathy takes hold with other team members. The product is being designed for SOMEONE. and people work with a purpose.

Now, some level-setting: just as the contrivance of having bad things happen to your hero in the first 10 pages of the movie script doesn't always work, the notion of propagating your personas to all your development team may not work either. But, in my experience, it's definitely work using it inside the UX circle, because the more you empathize with your well-rounded "characters," the better your product will end up be.

## Boot-strap usability testing: How to test your designs with little or no money

I've tested a LOT of different designs with users over the years, working in varying environments - from one extreme to the other. I've ran usability tests for companies who paid tens of thousands of dollars just to rent the (high-tech) facilities we used, and I've walked through design concepts with customer service reps in their break room. I've also helped set up three permanent usability labs, and through that process I've seen a lot of really expensive gear that several consultants said you "have to have" to really run an affective usability test.

To which, I say - Poppycock. Balderdash.

(I'd add another archaic term of disrespect, but I can't think of one right now - maybe later.)

Cost is not important- the testing is. "It's not that important, we don't need to test that," is a phrase I have heard repeatedly, sometimes from peers (who should know better). What I've found in my experience, the moment you have a high degree of confidence in a UI and think that you have "nailed" some design problem - that's the moment you HAVE to schedule a usability test, even if it's just with friends and family.

You may be completely right, the design may be utterly appropriate to the user task- but as a certain ex-President once famously said, "trust, but verify."

Usability testing is of vital importance to any design, and doing as many focused tests as you can afford results in a better end product. Of course, if you're an interactive design professional, I'm preaching to the choir here. You know that focused usability testing is important, and you are probably promoting usability testing to your project's stakeholders all the time.

Usability testing helps you validate that users can understand the interface you are presenting them, it gives you insight into the mental model of how users approach the task you are designing, and it lets you see the design from someone else's perspective. It also helps you fail fast, by making your mistakes in an early, non-production version of the solution you are implementing.

What you DON'T have, in many cases, is the

budget to do the testing you know should to get done. And even if you do have budget, in current economic conditions it may be - or has been - squeezed. And many outside of our domain look at usability testing as budget items that can be cut, not vital activities that help maintain quality.

I've been there, done that, got the t-shirt. So, how to get the same results you need, for less money? Here's some tips on cost cuts and strategies that will help get your tests funded and done.

(NOTE: In this article I refer to new designs, but the approaches I recommend are equally affective if you are testing existing systems to get "baseline" usability results.)

### Need users? Don't pay a recruiter, use Craig's List

This one is somewhat obvious, but worth noting. Craig's List is an awesome tool to get leads on ANY-THING, from used pool tables to replacement lamp shades. It can also help generate leads for potential participants for your testing. Keep in mind that, unlike a recruiter you pay to do the screening, this will mean that you need to screen the candidates yourself, so have a solid script/screener you can use.

I have actually had the misfortune of hiring recruiters who claimed they had an extensive database to pick candidate participants from- who used Craig's List to fill their slots. If you are comfortable doing the work (and have the time to dedicate to screening recruits)- cut out the middleman and do it yourself.

## Build your own reusable participant list

The more you test, the more opportunities you will have to meet different people in various professions that fits certain "niches" that you may need to revisit for future projects. If there are no "awkward moments" during the tests and the participants provide good feedback, then ask if they would be interested in coming back for future testing. If they are, add them to a "call-back" list you can go to later.

## Test a lot of stuff at once

Again, seems like a no-brainer, but worth considering. Several times I've "stacked up" a backlog of design concepts that do not need urgent consideration, some barely past the ideation stage. I don't set up specific targeted tests for this work, but the functional prototypes are "at the ready" whenever we have the time to expose them to users. If the dry run of the test protocol runs 45 minutes and you have the participants for an hour, bring them into the test.

## Interns rock - get some

If you have limited bodies at your disposal, contact a local university and get some more. Most colleges have intern programs that you can tap into, and you will often find some very passionate students that can help turn what was previously planned to be a short session with participants into a full test. Passionate, and cheap- a great combination.

## The cool software is nice, but usually unnecessary

Don't have the cool eyeball-tracking software from Facelab or great broadcasting/note taking tools like Morae? Don't sweat it. Get a cheap $300 mini-DV camcorder and a $20 tripod, position it next to the workstation (so the camera can pick up the screen or workspace as well as the participant) and hit record after you have the participant sign the video release (also, obviously, don't forget to have them sign the release).

Don't take notes yourself, focus on facilitating the test and following the protocol - you can take notes from the tape later.

Can't afford the camcorder? Get an intern to sit in the room and take notes. Again, they're cheap.

## When all else fails, use friends and family

It's never preferred, because you may have built up a personal relationship with the very individuals you may be walking through one of your designs, and biases will creep into their reactions. Get around this by e-mailing colleagues at your company and asking for volunteers - and, if possible, get one of your peers to facilitate the session if you are too close to the participant(s).

## Schedule the tests whenever the participants are available

We need to accept that people have lives, and,

while making sure that you get that design right under deadline (and, depending upon the project, under pain of torture) may be of MISSION-CRITICAL IMPORTANCE, the rest of the world doesn't care. So, be flexible - work with the participant's schedule. They are doing you a favor by coming out - never forget that.

## Don't cut the participant's compensation

One last note: don't try and save money on participant compensation. Pay them for their time and pay them well - I think $100 for an hour of a person's time is appropriate. Obviously, adjust based on your location, but make sure you pay better than minimum wage.

Hopefully, this has been helpful, and remember, TEST YOUR DESIGNS. It's important to do, even if you have no funding to do it. Test even if you don't have the approval - in my experience, it's always been easier to ask forgiveness than acceptance - especially easier after your usability test results in a better design to go to market with.

# Designing in an industry you don't know

I have worked with clients around the world, in multiple industries. When I was been brought in varied, depending on the project. Sometimes I came in before the project started and was tasked with planning out the UX approach and activities that would be appropriate (based on their needs and the type of project). Other times I came on as an individual contributor, doing specific tasks (such as research, design, etc.)

In both cases I often worked in a domain that I had no or little experience in. Here's some advice on how to engage and provide the most value if this is something that happens to you.

## Competitive Analysis

Evaluate any existing platforms that support the key activity around the solution that is being designed for, to inform a competitive analysis of what is done consistently and to identify best practices to leverage. I did a similar exercise for e-Government sites for the

Government of Egypt when I redesigned their e-Citizen portal last year (this competitive analysis is in my portfolio site, under Presentations).

I would try and get insights around what users would need from such a system, either through direct or indirect user research – I'd love to be able to watch users use a competing/similar platform to identify any usability issues they have (to avoid such issues in the solution I would envision). This may be a challenge to gain access to such users.

## Business Drivers

I would ensure that I had a good sense of the business drives for the solution – If I do not understand what the business drivers/KPIs for the solution I am designing are I would not be able to successfully implement a solution that aligns and supports these drivers.

## "Minimal Viable Documentation"

Create what I call "minimal viable documentation" of what the user journey and high-level experience would be – to get agreement from the key stakeholders and get a "green light" to support the detailed design work. This will include potential concept designs of key screens in the experience. Additionally, this journey map will drive detailed user stories used during the development process (which I will also help author). These design artifacts may be designed collaboratively in workshops based on the availability and interest of the stakeholders.

## Concept Design Creation and Testing

Create concept designs and a prototype to test the design with users – preferably collaboratively designed with the end users or representative stakeholders through a Design Thinking Workshop (which will also help you gain insights about the industry). Hopefully testing will be the actual users, though I may use "proxy" users who are stakeholders familiar with the processes to test the design with these users. User Centered Design is an iterative process, and so I would leverage the results to refine the design direction.

## Expectation Setting

Finally, during the entire process set expectations regarding the process and where I am throughout the process. If you are not familiar with the industry/domain then stakeholders might be extra "nervous" about your work. I like to "overcommunicate" and this helps insure alignment.

And make sure you have management support and clear direction. I always like to know where I stand, and I am not the work – if something in what I have designed is not working, the sooner I know the sooner it can be fixed. This is why the proper UX process is iterative, to support going from "first draft" to "finished novel. "

## What should an ideal User Experience Design lab have?

I've set up a couple of usability labs in my time, so I'll give you some of my advice/lessons learned in that space.

First the practical: get lots of wall space. I mean LOTS of wall space. Almost all the experience designers I have worked with love to use wall space to throw up mood boards, draft concepts, sketches, etc. Also, wall space is ideal for affinity exercises - and to that end get lots of stickies, markers and white poster paper.

Optimally you would have rolls of poster paper that you can mount towards the ceiling and then use to capture notes or a place to keep your stickies when you do brainstorming or analysis sessions.

You may also want to get dedicated project rooms, so you can keep all your work on the walls without having to move it from place to place. I've had to do analysis of data that was gathered through ethnographic research over a week-long period and switching rooms during that exercise was really frustrating and disrupted our workflow.

Now, hardware: use laptops, not desktops for your designers. The portability supports team members better. If you want to explore with next gen devices, get a touch computer like the ones HP has. If you really want to explore the space, get an Xbox and a PlayStation 3 and play with their new gestural devices/games. They are also useful for unwinding after the workday is done- as a famous starship captain once said, "The more complex the mind the more the need for play."

When it comes to usability testing, if you can set up a permanent lab, do so. The need for a two-way mirror is debatable, with all the teleconference software that exists. I personally think that building in wall or ceiling cameras and microphones is overkill- the participants know they are being recorded during a test, so why hide it?

Also overkill, in my opinion and experience, is eye-tracking software and hardware. A good facilitator or observer will be able to get the same or better insight than eye- tracking would. It may not have the level of specificity that the software would provide, but I think the data it provides is usually not very actionable.

If you are doing mobile design (and you should be) then get a variety of devices and hire someone who can develop in that space. There are ways to get designs on the devices without coding, but you may want to have the option to have more interactive mockups to test with. Get a monopod to lock a camera on a desk that can point down and record users using the device during testing (the smaller the camera the better).

And when it comes to usability testing software, there's a lot of great programs out there. The one I prefer is Morae, from TechSmith. It's Windows only but it does everything you need it to do: it captures the screen the user is using (or the video from an external camera, for when you are doing mobile usability testing) and the video of the participant (from a webcam) and also transmits the video via your local network to any other computer that has the Morae Observer software installed. It allows people to watch a test in near-real time from another room or even another building.

When it comes to design software, I love Omni-iGraffle for the Mac to do mockups, flow diagrams, mind maps, whathaveyou. I also love Axure RP to do designs and it generates functional prototypes you can use for testing. It's available for both Windows and OS X.

Finally, set up a lending library and invest in some of the best books in design you can find. Always keep learning.

## Usability testing: Should you test your own designs?

This is a topic of discussion that comes up in conversations with my peers about every six months or so. Should you test your own designs? Many, perhaps even the majority, say no- designers need to not facilitate usability testing of their own designs because of the potential bias that the designers bring. Others say it depends on what is being tested - for example, early concepts could be tested by the designer (because that is often more of a conversation than a strict task-driven test). Here's my opinion:

It depends.

I have tested my own designs in usability tests, both early formative tests and later summative tests, and I am well aware of the biases that a designer can bring to such an activity. Many times, you see users struggling with something you designed and it's hard to keep the emotions that produces in check (or, if the participant doesn't "get it," your frustration becomes a factor). This is where my training and background in journalism

comes in handy - you have to remain impartial and unbiased.

In many ways, you have to become Spock.

(Yes, I snuck a Star Trek reference in. I gotta be me.)

Spock had no "ego to bruise" and he never let his "passions be his undoing." When he encountered a situation he wasn't expecting he was not upset, he was fascinated. That's what I try to do - which is often a necessity, as budget and time constraints usually mean I have to design AND test for projects.

No, I've never been "perfect" and there have been some moments I "nudged" a participant, and I almost always recognize I'm doing that when it happens. Obviously, try and avoid that. As I've mentioned before, I try and avoid making my own mistakes and instead learn from other people's mistakes, and working at another company years ago I learned plenty when a usability test went very wrong.

The company had a really slick usability lab, with an audio/video control room that had multiple monitors that connected to the participants area. We were able to talk to the participant via a telecom system from the monitoring area as they interacted with designs we had installed on the computer set up for them. One day I was facilitating a

test of a design that a colleague had created- he had a passion about what he had done and was proud of his work.

Well, participant after participant continued to have issues with his design- they just did not "get" the information architecture he had implemented. My colleague got more and more frustrated and angry at what was happening with each test. Towards the end of the day, the last test subject, as others before her, encountered issues with the design. The designer was in the control room with me, and as I was talking to her through the intercom system the designer turned to another colleague and shouted "She's just stupid - they are all stupid. It's obvious! Can't they see it?!"

As my mike was STILL OPEN.

The participant, startled, asked "What?"

Needless to say, the test was over, and the designer never saw this design implemented (due to both the usability issues observed and the unprofessional behavior he demonstrated).

So, what's the lesson? If you're able to separate yourself from the design and can follow "the Vulcan way," then facilitating usability tests of your own work is possible. If you are too "wrapped up" in the work, then ask a fellow

UX colleague to do it. When it doubt, ask someone else to test your designs.

## You are probably wrong

After some years of doing this, I've realized that whatever you are designing, your initial draft... you are probably wrong.

User experience designers reading this shouldn't take this personally. We are, after all, extremely right most of the time - after all, you didn't get hit by a bus the last time you crossed the street, right? Otherwise you (probably) wouldn't be reading this. But when it comes to user experience and UI design, we are beholden to a harsh mistress - the end-user. And there's not just one of them.

Think of the millions of neurons that combine in a single human brain: all of those connections are formed based on biology, chemistry, and primarily. experiences. We are the sum total of our experiences, and our personalities reflect how the electrochemical reactions in our brain formed the self - our self - that exists in response to those experiences.

So, when you consider the millions of people

with different experiences and perspectives on life. you think you can figure out the optimal design for these people? A design that understands how they would all react to what you have presented? If you think so, well, you're wrong. You can get close - you can leverage the standards, conventions and cultural symbols that are shared in our country and use certain design patterns that people "get" but... you will not hit the mark the first time. Or maybe the second. Or maybe ever. But that's fine. Because you will never get it 100% right for every user, all the time.

I consider this idea- that you can't ever get it 100% right for everyone - as liberating. The best you can hope for is something that is obvious and good enough for the majority of people. It lets me look at design problems in a different way and explore and play and try different things. This is how you create new solutions... by trying something that has never been done before.

All to try and create something that makes a difference for users- something that is hopefully, after testing and refining, as right as you can get it.

## How do you articulate the business value of UX design?

It's tricky, but a key success metric is and always shall be one thing: money. Did the design, when implemented, save the company money (by reducing costs) or make the company money (by increasing sales of an item). I have found if you don't have "baseline" data to compare the new status quo you implement to the old then it's awfully difficult to prove the business value (you just don't have the data).

I've been fortunate enough to design and implement new solutions that "moved the needle" significantly- basically, the new version of the design I created, when implemented, showed improvements in the key metrics that the business was tracking against (customer satisfaction, time-on-task, and adoption/ uptake). In one instance I had a "hockey stick" uptick in adoption and customer satisfaction - the numbers jumped dramatically and stayed there. Why? Because the design I was replacing had pronounced usability issues, and the new design I created was markedly better and also was easy to understand, use and (a key factor) RE-use.

One other key success factor was I knew the goals of the design GOING IN - understanding the business drivers helped me form a happy balance between the business and the customer, which in turn allowed for a more effective solution. If you create a great design that doesn't support the business, you may produce a solution that is absolutely great.. but doesn't service the business's needs (which helps pay the bills, including the overhead that is, well... you).

Sherlock Holmes famously stated, "I cannot make bricks without clay." Facts- measuring of the before and after - are absolutely vital to speaking to the business. It may be "soft" numbers, like customer satisfaction or "net promoter score" - but it's still data that you can use to show the value of UX design.

### More on measuring success

Measuring success has become more and more important over the past few years. Net Promoter Score, or NPS, is a fairly good indicator, but it's "one-dimensional". No matter how many customers you survey it is still just a survey, without much context.

Some other ways you can get a sense of how customers think of (and just as important, use) your site or product:

Analytics can be a useful indicator, but not the way you might think. If you have any way of tracking through analytics how often the application is used it can give you some great insights into how your product or site is used. If customers tend to "go" to a particular "place" often this will tell you where to focus your attention. It also may help you identify potential pain points in your experience (I've used analytics to identify "drop off" points in an application process to make hat process better).

Social reputation is also a key indicator. Set up saved searches for your product name(s) in Facebook, Twitter and Google+ to monitor what customers are saying about your offerings. While not "scientific," it can give you some practical "real world" understanding.

Finally, have regular in-depth discussions with customers. Even if it's a group of 10 people, having a conversation where they discuss what they like and don't like about your site or application will give you insight into potential areas of improvement.

## How do UX Designers track their productivity?

When it comes to tracking productivity in UX design, the focus should always be on the outcomes, quality and hitting key milestones, and not on day-to-day activity.

Because there is no one "perfect" UX design process (just as there is no one perfect software development process) each project is going to have different timeliness and needs. One project may be heavy on detailed design documentation and is easier to "track" than one that is focused on user research and foundational understanding.

But even with a project that is "documentation-heavy", you have to be careful not to fall into the "to do list trap" of just crossing off things. Here's why: You can get all your design work done in a timely matter, but if the design sucks, who benefits? Certainly not the user, and definitely not your company. Yes, you will "look good" in the short term, in that management sees you are "hitting your dates" but you will be burned later if the design was rushed and ill-conceived. Trust me, I've been there.

How does an individual designer measure his own productivity? There are many different techniques I have seen and used, including the GTD methodology. But in the end, I think UX design isn't about "productivity" it's more about problem solving and making a difference for users. So, I look at satisfaction as a more important personal metric around my design work than the number of UI widgets I can crank out in a week.

As a design manager, how to track productivity? Well, in addition to the above, I make sure that the designers have time to refine, iterate, and fail. Yes, fail. We learn a lot by piloting early designs with users and finding out what doesn't work. Identify key milestones, let the designers follow the process that they are comfortable with, and focus on quality. Keeping in mind, of course, that deadlines are absolutely necessary as a motivator and a way to "focus the brain."

## How can a software company attract and keep great user experience designers?

As someone who has hired UX designers and also been brought in to implement UX design principles into a company (who had no understanding of the discipline), I have some opinions on this question. Here's the main one:

UX designers want to make a difference in users lives. Help them and let them.

We don't want to just punch a clock and take home a paycheck. We are ambitious. The most ambitious UX designers want to change the world. The more pragmatic ones want to make things better for users.

All of us want to make a difference.

So, how do you keep the best UX talent? Help us do that. Help us make a difference.

The way you can do this is, primarily, to support a user experience team and give them the time and the budget to let them do this. And make sure that they are aligned with product owners. No, correct that They should BE the product owners. They should work with the business management and negotiate the features and approach that is taken to roll out new features.

They should also be able to have the freedom to experiment and fail, and the culture of the company should embrace that failure as part of the journey and evolution of the company.

Basically, I'm describing the ideal company for someone like me go work in. If you have such a company that has as part of its core philosophy a customer-centered mindset, let's talk. You know where to find me.

# The Beginners Guide to Service Design

As I look at how the user experience design domain has evolved over the past few years, one thing has become very clear to me: Screens aren't that important anymore.

In the early days of UX, screens was a primary focus of design efforts, if not THE focus... because that was the key design deliverable everyone could agree upon. Stakeholders needed screens to review and approve, developers needed wireframes to code from, and users needed screens to interact with. Now, with technology such as voice and Internet of Things becoming more prevalent (and UI design conventions and standards maturing) a focus on screen design has been reduced.

What has become more pronounced and important is what I call "pure experience design": The definition of what users do and how they engage with the technology that empowers their lives. The best example of this type of "pure" design is the approach named Service Design.

Here's what I wrote a few years ago on Service Design:

*The service design discipline is about organizing people, processes, and technology to make sure the interaction between a company and its customers are as efficient and "positive" as possible. It is more than process design; in that it takes a user-centric look at everyone involved in the equation – the customers and the employees who are engaging them.*

Seeing the increased importance and value of this approach, I decided a quick "primer" on service design may be useful: Hence, this article. So, here's a beginner's guide to service design:

Clearly detail and document a "mission statement"

Before you begin, make sure that the team is all in agreement around what the goals and vision of the net new experience is. In most instances it will be a refactoring or improvement of an existing process, but in some cases, it may be a "blue sky/green field" project. Having this type of "mission statement" helps reduce ambiguity and put a "box" around the scope. For this primer let's look at it from the perspective of improving an existing process.

A good example: "Streamline the experience of selecting and picking up a rental vehicle from our company for high-value customers, to ensure that these customers have an experience that rewards their loyalty."

Document the existing process and technology

This involves user research and observation, as well as an analysis of all current process documentation and technology to understand all activities that take place. This informs the creation of service design blueprints (aka journey maps or experience maps).

Service design blueprints detail all process steps and this information is grouped in to two areas: "Front stage" or visible elements and activities, and "Back stage" or background activities and elements.

Carrying forward from our previous example/mission statement, you can look at all the interactions the customer has with the online system as well as support personnel at the car rental place as "front stage" and the back end databases and services (as well as the process of cleaning and refueling rental cars) as "back stage."

Here are the key details that a Service design blueprint should contain:

- Personas (or roles)

- Tasks/Activities

- Supporting processes

- Supporting materials (or job aids)

- Technology used (Devices and applications)

• Activity time/Time on Task (when available)

Identify the pain-points and areas of improvement

Now that you have a holistic document that details all the "moving parts" that is in the experience, you can look at the service design blueprint from the perspective of opportunity areas and pain-points. What tasks are redundant or can be improved through technology? What interactions can be "plussed" to make them more effective and provide a better experience to the user? Finally, what infrastructure changes can be made to improve the experience from both the customer and the employee's point of view?

As you can probably figure out, this is not about creating a new or different application but optimizing and improving the whole experience, for all involved. And by having this "big picture" perspective, you can start getting a good sense of the level of effort and potential cost of whatever change you come up with.

You may identify an idea such as a hand-written note to a customer with their 100th rental, and a gift. How would that be identified? How would the gift be delivered? Again, a good idea at this stage can be weighed against the total "bearing cost" of the idea, so that you can decide if it is worth the investment in tech and process changes. You can also "beta test" a new experience through user research and usability testing, to get a qualitative view of the change.

Document the change and scope

After validating the changes with stakeholders and users, you then revise the service design blueprint to reflect the new "desired" state. This new blueprint can then be an approval point with stakeholders and then will inform detailed requirements and documentation. And you have defined a "new baseline" for the experience – one that can be revisited and tuned as new technology comes to market months or years later.

Again, this is only a basic intro – for more details I recommend the great book This is Design Thinking. More details on this work is here: http://thisisservicedesignthinking.com.

## How a Design Thinking workshop can help create new experiences

In my many years as a user experience designer I have tried many different techniques and approaches to "kickstart" projects. After identifying what worked and what didn't, I "landed on" the Design Thinking workshop as my "go forward" strategy.

Design Thinking as an approach has been around for decades – the term was defined in 1969 and was formalized as an approach in the early 80s. Different people have varying "takes" on the process... Tim Brown from IDEO, in an article on the approach in Harvard Business Review, described it this way:

"(Design Thinking) is a discipline that uses the designer's sensibility and methods to match people's needs to what is technologically possible and a viable business strategy (to) convert into customer value and market opportunity."

Here's how I describe it:

Design Thinking is about defining a new experience through collaborative design. By understanding the business needs, applying empathy to understand end user's pain points and situation, and aligning and applying the best technology we are able to visualize and plan out that new experience and define the "art of the possible."

Over the past couple of years, I have facilitated many Design Thinking workshops with customers around the world. The typical goals of these workshops are:

Collaborate on defining "out of the box" innovative scenarios that can be applied in the experience

Identify opportunities where technology can be employed to "light up" these experiences

Define one to three target areas/experiences to inform the creation of a formal proof of concept/ project

The typical agenda is for a full-day session with key subject matter experts in the area being explored, as well as architects and technologists who can contribute to the conversation. The first part of the day is to discuss the current experience/pain points to get people to understand the domain being addressed. This then informs ideation around potential net new experiences for users. The second part of the day is around fleshing out these "candidate" experiences in more detail. The key is to activity facilitate the room and encourage creativity and collaboration… understanding that there will be different personalities at play and that negativity should be discouraged, especially in the second half of the day.

The outputs, at the very least, are "prototypes" of these net new experiences that can then be built out into full projects. These outputs can then inform scoping activities around what it would take to make the ideas real. Based on the specific project, there is flexibility around what we can do with the outputs – at the very least, it can lead to how current experiences can be incrementally improved through process revision or the application of new technology.

In the end, a Design Thinking workshop adds value even if the ideas that are generated are not viable or followed up on, because it increases everyone's knowledge of the area being discussed and (if properly facilitated) results in a collaborative design activity that is enjoyable for all participants. I co-lead a design thinking workshop for 200 people at a conference last year, and it was very well received and evaluated – almost everyone had a good time and engaged in the collaborative design activities.

Though if you aren't an experienced facilitator, I'd start with around ten people… You'll be much less exhausted.

# Finding the right balance: How UX and Agile can work well together

I've worked on many projects and several different software development teams in the past, and these teams have had great success in applying Agile best practices in their work. Unfortunately, the integration of UX processes into the Agile methodology is not always successfully achieved. Hence, here's my thoughts on how Agile and UX can best partner to produce features that customers use and love.

### Tactical: Setting the right balance

Many teams leverage UX resources only to inform product roadmaps set by product management – using research and testing to help decisions and set direction. In other cases, UX resources on Agile projects are effectively "order takers" – reacting to user stories and creating designs for development to support backlog items.

I think the best approach is to ensure UX is properly leveraged and balanced – equal partners in product management and the development effort.

When it comes to product management, UX-ers should partner with the Product Owner and product managers/stakeholders to ideate and new features and research customers to make certain the product backlog is driven by actual user needs. This, in turn, will inform the product roadmap – at least, an indicative one.

A key approach in this effort is to leverage Design Thinking Workshops to generate ideas that can be tested BEFORE any development work commences. This was the cadence I established for the Innovation Team I helped found at Fiserv (as well as how we worked with customers at Microsoft), and it was quite successful. New feature ideas, generated internally or through DT workshops, can be validated with users before they are formally added to the backlog.

Regarding development, we need be fully engaged in the sprint cycle – support development questions/asks, work one sprint ahead, and remove blockers that are UX related.

There are regular spikes that prevent development work from being estimated and completed – these are often UX related questions or areas that require user research and direction. Optimally these spikes can be worked on before they are estimated and built for the next sprint, and when it IS UX related Uxers should own that work.

Finally, during sprint planning and backlog grooming UX can partner with the whole team to identify focus areas that require design activities.

## Strategic: Building out standard capabilities and processes

In each team I've managed or mentored, I always tried to build a playbook of capabilities UX practitioners can bring to the product development lifecycle. Such a playbook would have details of the approach as well as specificity regarding dependencies, LOE, and deliverables.

Each capability UX can provide should be specifically detailed regarding:

• Description (what is the activity)
• Value proposition (why the activity is important)
• Resource Needs (How many UX people, partner resources, etc.)
• Timelines and Milestones
• Outcomes/Deliverables

This way expectations will be set properly for all – stakeholders, team member and the UX team. I always try and "timebox" each capability to no more than two weeks' worth of effort, to align with a typical sprint.

Some "candidate" capabilities:
• Design Review
• Accessibility Audit

- User Research – Interviews
- User Research – Ethnography
- User Research – Focus Groups
- Usability Testing

### Things to look out for

Getting executive buy-in: UX professionals need to focus on only the activities that will have the most impact when it comes to shipping a quality product. What is a quality product? One that increases revenue through improved usability and responding to actual customer needs. This will mean doing activities (such as research) that may not show an immediate benefit. You will need executive support to ensure that these activities can occur.

Resetting expectations: Doing high fidelity concept designs to get the PMs to sign off on a design is not the best use of anyone's time – and that is what is often done in Agile teams today. UX practitioners need to embrace "true" agile approaches at iterative designs and do detailed design AS NEEDED to support development of the right experience. We don't ship wireframes or Sketch files – we ship code.

Content strategy: Content (help copy, tips, feature descriptions) is a core part of any experience. Any UX Team also need to properly partner with the people doing this work to ensure we can influence this content in a positive way.

# Essays

*Thoughts on the user experience domain and discipline, as well as essays on technology, trends and the future.*

## My background, and how it prepared me to work in user experience

I'm lucky, in that I've done a LOT of different things - and I think that variety of experiences has helped me become better at... Well, user experience.

It all started in a 5,000-watt radio station in Birmingham, Alabama. With just a $50-a-week paycheck and a dream... No, seriously, Ted Baxter references aside, one of my first real jobs was in radio. I did college radio and, for a while, overnights for the local rock station. Doing a job like that taught me the importance of organization and multitasking, and, most importantly... Communication. If you didn't fill that dead air, it was exactly that... Dead air. A lot of my communications skills can be attributed to me being behind a "hot mike" and trying to both communicate and entertain.

I also had a passion for design, and at the time the notion of the domain that eventually became known as "user experience" didn't exist, so I learned graphic design and worked doing magazine layouts and advertisements for sporting periodicals such as Bowhunter and Deerhunter Magazine. It wasn't glamorous, but I learned how to flow text around images and present things in a creative way.

For a while I managed a record store for a Kentucky- based chain, and that helped me get a sense of the practical realities of a segment of the business world that allowed me to communicate to business people with a better understanding of where they were coming from.

I then learned about this crazy new thing called "The Internet" and taught myself how to code HTML and make web pages, a skill that came in handy when I started working for a web service company that was a huge opportunity for me to learn about EVERYTHING: database design, server configuration, uptime, DNS tables, web security, e-commerce... The works.

You may notice that I have not yet described my formal education... And there's a reason for that. I learned more by working and doing than I ever did in college, though I attribute what I learned when I majored in Journalism with a lot of my skills in usability testing, listening, writing, and objectivity.

So, when UX finally became a domain of note, I was ready... It was the perfect fit for what I had learned and done - it was about something I was always good at - designing solutions for users and solving problems.

## Technology, applied: understand how people use tech and then support their needs

Let's go back in time a bit - back in time to those carefree days of yore, when tech companies piled new feature after new feature into each consecutive release of their flagship products. When each new release promoted a new shopping list of goodies to entice eager buyers to upgrade.

Remember all that? Because those days are long gone. Dead, and buried. The new rules of engagement? Not more features, but better features. Improvements, enhancements, and usability. Now the experience the technology provides- how it does something, not what it can do - has come into fast focus.

Why? Because companies who focus on user needs and providing the most affective experience are thriving, and companies that are stuck with "featuritis" are barely keeping up.

My job is in the domain and discipline of user experience design- which consists of creating meaningful and useful solutions that make sense for our users. It is a focus that is becoming more and more important in our new user- centered reality. Here's some recommendations on how to leverage technology to support your customer, in this new "features as commodity" age.

### Focus on how users use technology, not the technology itself.

We recently did a mobile research study, to understand how people use their mobile devices- and a key indicator we focused on was the engagement and involvement people had with the mobile technology. Learning how they think of the devices, and the usage patterns and mental models we defined, allowed us to better understand what users need to define the right offerings.

Understand how people leverage technology to make their lives better, and you will find key opportunities to engage with your customers in places and spaces you may have never considered before.

Features are important, but how they are implemented is even more important. As mentioned earlier, now the programs are designed for users, and not by engineers or project managers trying to one-up the competition. Now, the software is appropriate, appealing and most importantly USEFUL.

## What do your customer think about technology? Or do they think about it at all?

Your customers are not, for the most part, techies. They are surrounded by technology almost every minute of the day, but they don't think about it. They know what they like, and like what they know. If new technology enters their life it does so organically, and they only adopt the new if it is obvious, nonthreatening and kind. Yes, I said KIND. We need to bring a tone and an approach to our service offerings that are humanistic in nature, not just technically impressive.

Understand that technology is a tool, not an end to itself. If you are focused on technology in your job, keep this in mind. And that you may be in a tech "bubble" and that the way you think of this space is not the way most people do.

## Empower users with technology, don't hobble them.

Every touchpoint with your customers is either supported or enabled by technology. Whether it's a customer calling your support line or a user of your online site, technology is the mechanism that allows the communication to happen. Make sure that the experience is one that supports your customers and doesn't frustrate them. In the days of immediate customer feedback loops, through social media, the more you empower your customers the more they will like your company and its offerings. And the more they will recommend them to their friends and family.

# Saying goodbye to the UX echo chamber

I've spoken at a number of UX design conferences in the past, though it's been a while. The past two years my proposals have been consistently rejected, the latest being a rejection of all three of my proposed panels by UX Australia. I've rationalized this rejection in various ways – I'm not a well-known "name", my proposal wasn't strong, my ideas weren't original or appropriate to the audience… but I've moved past rationalization.

I'm now no longer going to try.

I spent some time asking myself – why did I want to speak at conferences in the first place? My introspection revealed that it was because I wanted to be on stage, the center of attention. It was less about wanting to share and teach and present my ideas and more about building my reputation… and stroking my ego. Not to say that I have matured past that (all creative types are self-centered) but at least I'm conscious of my own motivations.

I've also slowly, over time, changed my opinions about design conferences. I think that design conferences are now more of an echo chamber than anything else, with everyone nodding and agreeing to the same thing. The user experience field has matured, and the point of these conferences isn't about convincing anyone on the value of UX – we all "get it". The maturity of our discipline means that presentations… well, they are less about education and more about self-congratulation and ego – obviously, many of these people are motivated to speak for the same reason I have been.

Design conferences are now more like science fiction conventions than a learning opportunity (and trust me, I've been to several conventions – I know of what I speak). And there's no debate anymore: any contentious conversations are at the edges around trivial matters like eyeball tracking software – it's like Star Trek fans debating whether Kirk or Picard would win in a fight.

Another thing that has turned me off of design conferences (and is a long-term threat to the growth of UX) is that there is an arrogance shared by many UX designers I've met… especially with many of the "superstar" speakers.

It's one thing to know how to do your job, and do it well, it's quite another to think you have all the answers. This attitude is not only unattractive and off-putting, but it lacks in the one thing we UX folks must always have: humility.

I'm very concerned that ours is becoming an industry of pride & arrogance instead of one about learning, understanding & helping users. I never want to think I know how people think and am always "right". The discovery of how people live, and how we can make their lives better – that is where I always want to be. And speaking at conferences, presenting myself as if I have all the answers... well, as I stated above, that's not who I am.

To paraphrase the second law of thermodynamics, energy is neither gained nor lost – it is merely transferred. So instead of chasing the public speaking gig at design conferences and will instead be focusing my energies on my discipline (and a book – maybe). I will still attend conferences when I can, primarily to network and keep my skills.

Finally, if I do present, I want to do it where it matters, where I can make a difference – industry conferences where I can convince bankers, manufacturers, and corporation decision-makers about the value of user experience design. I want to share my ideas on how user-centered design can change their businesses, help their customers and, in the end, make them money. I want to "evangelicise" UX to people who don't get it – those are the people I want to speak to.

And, hopefully, make a difference.

# Why UX is more than "making something pretty"

I've seen a frustrating trend lately regarding how many outside of user experience teams think of the discipline. Their opinion may be simply ignorance or may have been influenced by how UX folks on our side "sold" themselves (or the capability). This opinion is one-dimensional: They leverage UX practitioners to create visual designs, storyboards, etc. to help in "storytelling" a "net-new" experience to sell customers.

This activity in-and-of itself is fine, and if it can help "close" deals so much the better – but when we UXers do such "fit and finish" work, we are usually not involved in defining the new experience to be visualized. Either we come in too late or not even considered as needed to help craft such an experience. Not taking advantage of UXers to define such an experience is, as Spock said in Star Trek II, a "waste of material." That's the whole POINT of being a UX practitioner, after all.

## Leveraging the full "UX Stack"

Applying a user-centered design approach to a project – be it a new app, work flow, or BOT – means you bring the right people, at the right time – especially the right UX folks. You need UX practitioners to do more than just create pretty pictures. The best use of UX talent in a virtual/ blended team is to investigate, envision and validate the new experience – optimally before any code is written or any requirements are locked in. These activities can still occur in the aforementioned sales cycle – even though it would be in a limited "time-boxed" way.

The reasons why to do this work should be self-apparent (though to many it is not): UX teams focus on the user, on how they work and what they do – and by doing so you determine the best possible feature set to serve the needs of these users. When you skip this type of "due diligence", you do so at your peril.

I should know, because I have been on the outside-looking-in at projects where UX was engaged solely in the aforementioned "fit and finish" effort during the sales cycle, and when the project starts there is no engagement of the UX team. The frequent outcome that results is the creation of a solution looking for a problem that no one needed solving, and a failed initiative.

I've also seen UX engaged on projects where

we do "only" X – be it design reviews, research, or design documentations. Supporting projects with a single-threaded effort or work product (wireframes, storyboards) helps the individual's person's reputation (and builds their body of work/portfolio), but the opportunity to have deeper integrated engagements usually stops at such an activity.

The problem is these single threaded activities can be perceived as "optional" or "nice to have" (more and more the case as Enterprises move to an agile methodology vs. traditional "Waterfall" development). This results in the UX team being viewed as a cost-center instead of an investment in making sure the solution is appropriate for and desirable by the end-users.

Bringing the full "UX Stack" (research, ideation, testing, and design) to projects – and showing the value of these activities in real world project motion – means that a UX team will never be considered optional…. And the resulting experience will be better suited to help people do and achieve more.

### Leaving UX to experienced practitioners

Even worse, I'm also seeing some teams think that they don't NEED to partner with any UX team, because they assume (sometimes correctly, other times not) that the work done by the UX team can be done "in house" by themselves or their peers, or "farmed out" to a partner. Yikes.

I'm all for non-UX practitioners leveraging the tools and techniques that a UX "toolkit" brings... but I'm not OK with people thinking that they could do the whole "UX Stack" themselves... or paying the lowest bidder to "check the box" to keep costs low.

## Closing

Maybe it's just me, but as I see UX becoming more and more important across the Enterprise, I see a big risk when UX is just perceived as a visual/UI design activity. We have to do better at communicating what the full and rich capabilities of UX is, otherwise the key capabilities and value we bring to the table will wither on the vine... And products and services will become less and less accessible and usable by consumers.

## The commoditization of UX

Let's go back in time a bit – over a decade ago. Macworld, 2007. Steve Jobs stood before a crowd of True Believers and revealed not just one, but THREE revolutionary new products. A new, Innovative wide-screen iPod. A next-generation mobile phone. And a breakthrough Internet device.

Of course, he was talking about one product: the iPhone. I was working for Cingular Wireless at the time, and before this product was released, we were selling Razr phones like hotcakes. Less than a year later we couldn't give them away. I think anyone reading this could easily understand why. The iPhone set a new standard to the way mobile phones worked. It did more, it was simple to learn and elegant to touch. It was designed with the user and usability in mind, and that, combined with an amazing industrial design, made the iPhone markedly better than any other device on the market. It was no contest.

It is amazing. Eleven years later, to watch and hear people in the audience gasping at some moments

– visual voice mail, satellite images on maps, etc.

Which is why Apple is in trouble. They aren't making people gasp anymore.

Apple recently announced it was reducing sales projections, in part due to reduced demand in China. But the sales in the US and other parts of the world has been soft as well. Why? Many pundits have pointed to the higher price points of the latest models as well as economic factors. I think the answer is simpler than that.

The UX has been commoditized.

What was once an exceptional user experience on the iPhone has become – well, just like what you get on any Android. The new features that have been introduced the past few years were either copied by Google for their Android OS or copied FROM the Google-based phones. Manufacturers such as Samsung have produced very slick well-designed handsets that are equal in build quality to iPhones. And while they are usually cheaper than the iPhone, the reason why people buy them is not price – remember the first iPhone was VERY expensive compared to other smart phones.

No, the reason why the iPhone sold so well and the reason why it's not doing so now is there is barely any difference between smart phones in 2019. Why pay a premium price for an experience that is not only just like other cheaper phones, but also an experience that is not any better than your two-year old phone?

And it's not just smart phones. When you look at web apps and desktop operating systems, we have reached a point of parity and maturity. There is not much uniqueness left. (I've written about this before).

So, what is Apple to do? What should all the UX designers focus on? As always, I go back to the core element of an effective user experience: The users. Understand what they need, how they use these devices, and spend time investing in a robust ideation cycle for your product to identify what new features will really excite them. Break out of the commodity game and bring you're a game.

Samsung will be trying to do that by rolling out smart phones with a hinged screen the next two years – no doubt Apple is also thinking about something similar. If it was me, I'd do the unexpected: put out an "iPhone classic". Use the same form factor as the first device that Steve Jobs brought the world, and take advantage of all the great advances since (and the larger interior space the device has) to bring users 24 hour battery life, the great camera and speed that is in newer devices, and also one more thing – a "breakthrough" app that makes people gasp again.

And then sell it for $499. They'd make billions.

## The Cambrian Explosion of UI Design (and where we are now)

"How do you use this?"

Whenever any new piece of technology is released, this is the core (usually unspoken) question that consumers of said technology have. How does it work? What does it do? The better designed devices and applications build in affordances and familiar controls that allow users to pick up on how to engage and use it – the tech that doesn't build in these helpful elements produces frustrated users and reduced adoption.

We have come a long way from the technology that I started using in the early 1980s – the early computers such as the Commodore 64 or the Apple II had a character-based UI and taking full advantage of the hardware meant becoming very familiar with the spiral-bound manual that came with these units. I love watching videos of the "8-Bit Guy" on YouTube as he takes us through some of this "ancient" tech.

Today, including a manual for a piece of hardware or an application is rare, not just because companies want to save money on packaging, but because computing devices and programs either have help built in or they are designed with the aforementioned affordances in mind (or both).

Mobile applications were especially lacking in help or support documentation. With so many simple "single-purpose" applications that existed on early smart phones, there was no need to have any help options due to the limited functionality

Except... for a long while, every app LOOKED DIFFERENT.

In the early days of mobile applications (kickstarted by the popularity of the iPhone), developers took full advantage of the platform to create games and apps that were wildly different from each other. Even though Apple provided design guidelines and UI element libraries, many apps had its own custom interaction models and controls... Which meant users had to "relearn" how to use each app. When Google's Android devices arrived a couple of years after the iPhone a similar situation occurred, compounded by the fact that the Android OS had different "core" interaction patterns from iOS devices.

I consider this "early period" of mobile apps the "Cambrian Explosion of UI Design."

Here's the Wikipedia description of the Cambrian Explosion:

*The Cambrian explosion, or less commonly Cambrian radiation, was the relatively short evolutionary event, beginning around 542 million years ago in the Cambrian period, during which most major animal phyla appeared, as indicated by the fossil record.*

The Cambrian Explosion of UI design (both at the application and the mobile OS level) resulted in a lot of fantastic applications, elements and interaction models – and also a lot of really unusable confusing applications. The result was a consolidation and "smoothing out" of the mobile experience – Apple and Google refined and started enforcing their standards, weeding out badly designed applications. App designers started following the conventions more, and finally both iOS and Android started looking more and more "alike" when it comes to the core interaction patterns. Now, usability and learnability has improved for all devices and applications, though the occasional "divergent" application still comes out on a regular basis.

A similar situation has occurred on the web and with desktop operating systems, with Microsoft, Google and Android's OSs looking more alike than different in most respects.

That's where we stand today. Everything is different, yet everything looks pretty much the same. Is this good or bad? It depends on how you look at it. Having standards that have organically come to exist that Ui designers can follow allows for quicker adoption and understanding, but such standards can also constrict creativity and innovation. In my opinion, the overall result is better than bad, as designers should focus more on user needs than how calendar controls should render.

However, I'm getting pretty tired of seeing the hamburger menu.

# How to Avoid "UX Theatre"

I've been involved in a lot of projects in my many MANY years as a UX professional – some good, some bad, most... interesting. One thing I'm beginning to see as a trend is the rise of what I consider "UX Theatre". That is when project stakeholders and product owners give a generous amount of attention to user experience when they are talking about the project, but when it comes to the actual motion of DOING the actual user-centered design WORK... well, they always find a reason not to actually make that activity occur.

I wish I could take credit for the term, but I am not that smart – the real credit comes from @spydergrrl on Twitter:

*Spent the weekend thinking about how a few projects I've come across recently are doing UX theatre, not actual user-centered design. Sadly, it's becoming more prevalent as execs learn the term UX, but their teams aren't empowered to do all the work that UX entails.*

Sometimes, it's really frustrating. I know of one project that had FOUR design teams, across multiple locations – dozens of designers – but the project had only ONE researcher, who did nothing but test designs to validate them. As our current President might tweet… SAD.

So, here's how to recognize UX Theatre, and hopefully avoid it.

### Little-to-no user research

When you have product owners who think they know better than the actual users, you will often see some very direct comments from such people around what the users "want." They will be absolutely right about their opinions and expect no one to question their all-seeing all-knowing wisdom.

These "experts" lead their teams down a single-threaded path that results in a myopic offering that will, more often than not, result in an offering that solves no one's problems.

The way to avoid this, of course, is to put aside bias and actually go out and talk to the end-users of the offering, to identify how the solutions solve the real problems.

Of course, such motion means that these product owners will have to relinquish control… which, for egotistic product managers, mean they will have to relinquish power.

## Stolen ideas, rationalized

"Great artists steal." When you hear people quote Picasso, be wary. It is an excuse to take shortcuts and not innovate.

This is not saying that reuse of standard patterns is a bad thing – it IS saying that designers who lift features and interaction patterns wholesale are potentially taking shortcuts and not really designing anything. It's not innovation, it's copying features from other more successful apps.

## No usability testing

Testing interactions and designs is UX 101, and any project team that decides that they "don't have time" to do these activities end up with an experience that is always less than perfect. The idea that any designer can get it right the first time is egotistical and inflexible. User feedback is a GIFT – not taking advantage of it in early design iterations is a mistake that will cost the project in the long run.

## A focus on visual design, instead of interactions

As important visual design is as part of an experience, it is NOT the key focus of any experience design effort. The focus should be first on user needs and pain points, and after that – the way users interact with the information and the functions provided. When you have multiple teams focusing on branding and not on HOW the user gets things done, you are setting up a very large stage to perform "UX Theatre."

## Pretentious conversations that go nowhere

How important is design? So important that you have to spend HOURS discussing it. When you are on a project that has multiple workshops to identify how to make a widget work, and what verbiage should be used for a particular control, congratulations! You are a featured player in a "UX in name only" exercise. You will burn many hours without solving any meaningful problem. Great if you are a consultant paid by the hour, horrible if you make to want a meaningful difference in people lives.

## Tweaking minutiae that doesn't matter

How does that calendar control work? How do people submit their time on a mobile device? When you spend effort on details that are inconsequential you are focusing on the wrong level – you solve the problems that don't make a real difference. As thermodynamics shows us, energy is neither gained nor lost – it is merely transferred. Invest the time in solving the "big rock" problems instead of the inconsequential ones.

There you have it – some indicators that you are may be playing "UX Theatre" instead of making a difference in what your team is producing. In case of UX Theatre, apply ample user research and feedback and use that achieved wisdom to solve the real problems – and make users lives better.

# On Discoverability and Learnability, where Apple doesn't "just work"

A couple of months ago the New York Times features a very interesting article discussing the newest features that were being added to Apple's iOS devices. More an op-ed than a news story, the piece interviewed developers and end user of some of the features, and made the case that the features... well, aren't easy to use or find. Here's the key quote:

"A lot of people will think it's their fault, and it's really the designer's fault. People want apps to be easy to use."

Apple isn't the only one who gets dinged – Google also gets criticized for its confusing (and now-abandoned) Google Plus social service.

Putting my UX designer "hat" on, I can see that the issues detailed in the NYT piece is two-fold: First, the new features are hard to find and that lack of discoverability is reducing use – which in turn impacts developers who try and plug into and monetize these features (A similar problem exists with the Apple app store – finding apps using just the category navigation is laborious). I think the best example of this, and one not mentioned in the article, is the 3D Touch feature Apple rolled out a couple of years ago, where people reveal app options by pressing and holding down on the icon of the app – because there is no visual cues, many users never even know the functionality exists.

Second, many of the new features described (once found) are not that easy or obvious to use. This is also impacting adoption and increasing user frustration. A good example is the Apple Watch UI, which has had a major redesign of its interface to respond to some of these issues. For a company that has famously claimed their products "just work", these types of issues should not happen – or they should be rare.

This is not saying that my former company (Microsoft) doesn't have similar issues... It's a challenge the product team faces with each new release of Windows and Office, and it doesn't always successfully solve these problems. However, Microsoft has never had the level of braggadocios marketing and messaging Apple rolls out on a regular basis.

What are the root causes of these two issues? Well, it's something that people at my company knows very well – "featuritis." Apple's facing a big challenge when it comes to their iOS devices... The products are mature, and (in my opinion) feature complete. How do you make people buy new versions of the same product they have, a product that (ironically) "just works" fine? You add more features. And you can't completely redesign the UI every year, because that will throw a steep learning curve at many of your users not to mention annoy the power users who have become quite adept at the existing interface.

So, what should Apple do? What should any company do when it comes to this problem? Here's some suggestions:

## Design an extensible UI architecture

When the product or application is first being designed, make sure that the foundational UI architecture can stretch and scale to support future features. A good way to do that is to not put artificial limits on navigation options, as well as making sure that the "design language" leveraged is easy to learn and aligned with standards users are accustomed to. This is easier said than done, especially when you have a rushed production schedule... but this "firm foundation" will allow you to build out a much better long-term experience.

## Have a clear simple use case for every feature

Who is the new feature intended for? What problem or task is it trying to support or solve? Having a clear use case, one that can be describe in a simple sentence, allows you to develop a feature that makes sense to the laymen user and add value. "With this feature, you can order pizza using emojis" is a simple, somewhat clear use case... but it doesn't make a lick of sense. How is this better than using a saved order or a quick menu?

Finally, any use cases defining a new feature should be researched with users to confirm they are truly "helping" the end user.

### Align new functions with similar (existing) ones

By grouping "like features" this helps user discover new ones, because they will be trying to accomplish tasks aligned with the new functionality. It's as simple as that… You can also add a quick "NEW" indicator next to the new feature that links to a small description.

### Don't be afraid to kill a "bad" feature before shipping

Many writers use the phrase "kill your darlings" when editing their work – in order to make a story or an article tighter and more effective, you cut out the fat… even if those words, sections or characters may be the author's favorites. Designers and product managers should think about new features the same way – if they don't work, then cut them out. It's better to renege on promises to users than to ship a feature that is ill-conceived and leads to a bad experience.

### Tell users what's new

This one is obvious, but Apple tends to roll out OS updates with very little online-help or documentation. Only a couple of screens at start-up detail new features, and even then, the detail is sparse.

The best way to do this is (as noted above) is to flag the new feature with some indicator, and then link to information about the new feature… preferably video, which shows how the new functionality works.

So, there you have it – five suggestions on how to make your features discoverable and learnable. I hope these ideas can help… and hopefully Apple will leverage similar ideas to make their products better for all users.

# Creating a User Experience SWAT Team

If you are a member of a user experience design team, you are probably very busy right now. UX design is in high demand many companies have finally realized that a focus on design and the user experience is the "secret sauce" that improves customer satisfaction, increase sales, and generally separates their offerings from the competition.

But with this increased demand often comes increased pressure- multiple projects and multiple stakeholders vying for the same limited resources. How to cope? Well, I have started to adopt some methods that will (hopefully) allow me to grow a UX "SWAT Team" that can better adapt and deal with such demands.

SWAT, as you may know, stands for special weapons and tactics, and SWAT teams perform high-risk operations normal police officers are not equipped to handle.

Therefore, I think of UX" SWAT team" as one that can be pulled into any situation, execute quickly and effectively, and then quickly move on to another project. Here are the methods that I am applying to set my team up for success:

## Know your limitations - and define the rules of engagement

I've seen many projects where the roles and responsibilities of the project were ill-defined, and the project went on and on and on... Don't let that happen. SWAT teams always have clear objectives and define who does what when - not having such coordination could cost lives. While a UX project usually doesn't have such high stakes, not having the rules of engagement defined will usually lead to unneeded stress, missed deadlines and miscommunication.

Take the time to form your plan and define EXACTLY what your team will do to support the project. And don't overdo it - find out exactly what deliverables the stakeholders need and provide them - don't spend two weeks producing a findings document when developers need design specifications.

## "Specialization is for insects"

The above is one of my favorite quotes, from author Robert A. Heinlein, and one that I have tried to apply in my own life. The idea behind it is simple- be good at many different disciplines instead of being great at only a handful of things. Having a UX team filled with people with varied skills allows you to react to the needs of any new project much better than if you have a team who only does one or two things well.

## Get Things Done

I'm a big David Allen fan, and Allen's Getting Things Done action management method has been incredibly useful to me and several of my colleagues. If only some of Allen's approaches are applied across your UX team you will see a marked increase in productivity - and a significant reduction in stress.

### Test quickly, and test often

If you are revising an existing design, do informal usability tests as soon as you can, even if it's with friends and family - to get sense of the "baseline" of the system. It will give you much-needed context - or "intel" - to see what design challenges you may be facing. Then test again - even if it's thin wireframes sketches. Finally, interview end users as soon as you can, even if it's by phone, to understand their perceptions and needs.

### Use the right tools (as applicable)

I'm a big fan of the Axure rapid prototyping tool, which allows you to both mockup UI designs and document them - if you have not tried it, you can download a demo from axure.com. But you shouldn't tie yourself to this (or any) tool if it doesn't work for you - you should be focusing on the design problem, not the process of figuring out how to make things happen in a software program. Use paper, pencil, and whiteboards to iterate and ideate quickly.

## Over-communicate

Never operate in a vacuum- always keep project stakeholders in the loop, even if you don't think they need to be. At worse, they will ignore your e-mail updates. but I have found that more often than not such constant communications increases confidence in the abilities of your team and whatever results they produce. Over-communicate internally as well, to make sure everyone knows who is doing what and that they are on the "same page."

## Use the Scotty method of estimation

NEVER underestimate how long it will take to do something. apply the Scotty method. Scotty (from Star Trek, of course) always overestimates and then... well, just read this chunk of dialogue:

Kirk: "How long to re-fit?"

Scotty: "Eight weeks. But you don't have eight weeks, so I'll do it for you in two."

Kirk: "Do you always multiply your repair estimates by a factor of four?"

Scotty: "How else to maintain my reputation as a miracle worker?"

Kirk: "Your reputation is safe with me."

# Where does "doing" happen?

I recently tested some designs for my company and thought that a screen design I came up with (a UI module that gives users better visibility into their finances - in a sense, "how are things going?") was rock solid.

It was building on a couple of earlier iterations of the design and I considered the testing to be a mere formality.

Boy, was I wrong.

Testing began, and before I showed the first participant the design in question, I exposed the participants to other designs in the prototype system, screens which allowed them to move money around and do things. Then, I got to that "how are things going?" screen.

Blank stares. Confused looks. EPIC FAIL.

Whenever you have to explain to a participant how something works when they can't, after some consideration, you tell yourself "well, you see that big thing on the wall over there? It's called a drawing board, get back to it."

(And, obviously, the majority of your users will not have the opportunity to have a tall bald man sit next to them and tell them how stuff works- though anything could happen).

After seeing the same reaction occur, again and again, with the remaining participants it became pretty obvious the design was NOT "rock solid" and in fact had some significant issues. What was simple and obvious to me, the designer, was not at all to the participants, who all represented typical users of the existing system. Again, this is why you test designs with users (probably preaching to the choir, but still).

After analyzing their responses and the notes my lab partner took, I discovered a major problem with the design. It was intended to be "interactive" in that, if you saw a data point on this screen that was a cause for alarm, you could click it, open the item, and change it. The participants did not see this AT ALL. They thought, due to the location of the screen in the navigation structure and the content surrounding this design that the screen was only a helpful "report" = Informational, NOT functional.

Why? Well, it was because the navigation structure that was applied in the proposed design. The UI modules that supported the primary functions (moving money around) were on other pages... the participants expected that they

needed to go to one of those pages if they saw something "wrong" instead of doing it on the page itself.

In other words, the participants separated the system into two spaces: the "doing" space and the "reviewing" space and mixing them in this screen caused an unexpectedly high amount of confusion.

How to fix this? Well, I'm still working on it, but a possible solution is to place a smaller, more streamlined version of the "how are things going?" module on the functional pages, as "thermometer" to help users understand their current situation (and making sure to not duplicate functionality that already exists).

This was a good reminder to me, and hopefully you, kind reader, to remember: Every screen, like a scene in a movie script, should have a point to it, a purpose, to help support the goals of the user. What I did was the UI design version of mixing a dialogue-heavy exposition scene with a big action sequence. it was a muddled mess. Live and learn.

## Zen and the art of user experience design

Simplicity matters.

I can't even count the number of times I have tried to do something in a software program and the process of attempting the task at hand was either needlessly complicated or hard to find or both. I almost used the word "confronted" in that last sentence, because that's what it felt like - conflict. The program was not working with me, it was fighting me - using controls and ideas that an engineer had conceived, one that was alien to me as a use.

I do not want to fight software - I want to USE software.

As a user experience designer, I hope (and pray) to never inflict the type of contrived and ill-informed program on my users- that's why I do my "due diligence" and research users, test my designs, and make the best solution I can for my company's customers in the (always limited) time I have to deliver such a solution. And, in those times I find limited - which is more often than not - I follow two basic principles.

Wabi and Sabi.

What, you may think, is that? Well, they are two concepts of simplicity as defined in Zen. I approach these concepts as a designer, not with any pretension or formal focus, but as guiding principles. I make the design simple and try and make it effortless for the user to take and use. My designs will never be perfect- nothing is.

I always focus on the saying I heard many years ago that "perfect is the enemy of good," and so always try and I make the design appropriate and approachable more than anything else, using the language of the user and not some contrived technical terms or making the screen oppressive and, therefore, intimidating.

It isn't easy, and I'm still working on it, but I definitely recommend that you take the concepts of Zen to heart whenever you approach a design problem. The simple path is sometimes far better than the complex one.

# What makes software elegant?

Elegance is in the eye of the user.

I state that because the perception of elegance is a personal one, and the best you as a designer can do is define what you think elegance is and then provide a solution that meets that definition. So, here's my definition of what makes software elegant:

It gets out of the way. Elegant software provides an interface that supports the user's primary tasks and doesn't clutter or abstract the tools the user needs to accomplish the task. It is simple, obvious, straightforward and requires very little intellectual effort to understand immediately. It can be a stock tracker, a game, a word processor Anything, as long as it is designed with a focused intent.

It is designed intelligently and thoughtfully. If there is a hierarchy of controls, the core functions are right up front, and the secondary controls are available at a level beyond the first. I had one of my best design reviews ever when a key stakeholder just absolutely ripped one of my designs apart, because it did not present the controls in a thoughtful way. "it looks like you just threw a bucket of buttons on the screen," He said, and he was right. Elegant design is thoughtful design.

It speaks the same language as the user. You can design a screen for an airline pilot that will totally not work for a registered nurse, and vice-versa. Elegant design should be focused on the user and their particular needs and speaks their language. Design that tries to be all things for all people inevitably ends up being bad. understand your user, support their needs, and do it using the terms and conventions that work for them.

One last thought: elegance does not necessarily line up or align with delight. The emotion of delight can be triggered by many things, and you can provide an elegant solution that does not provoke delight. If anything, the ability to provoke delight is getting harder, as the baseline of user expectations continue to rise as they are exposed to ever more refined technology.

Delight is hard, and elegance can provoke delight. Sometimes.

# UX's Greatest Secrets, Revealed!

I'm a big fan of Penn and Teller and have been for many years. I saw them live for the first-time last month and was blown away by their performance.

What I really love about Penn and Teller is that they often "pull back the curtain" and reveal how they do their magic. Other magicians produce an air of mysticism and pretense around their craft, but Penn and Teller will have none of that. They know they are playing tricks, fooling the audience, and by letting everyone in on what they are doing they debunk mysticism while also (hopefully) teaching you something.

Their attitude towards their work inspired me to write an article that hopefully "pulls back the curtain" on some of user experience design's "greatest mysteries." Much like Penn and Teller's mocking of "artists" like Criss Angel, I have met quite a few pretentious design types in UX who think way too much of themselves and what they do. This type of attitude frustrates me, because much of what UX professionals do is actually easy to teach and apply.

That's why I write about UX: to demystify the domain and make it accessible to all. To that end, here are some of the key "secrets" of UX.

## We aren't all-knowing prophets

I know many UX designers present themselves as unquestionable experts on human beings; as seers whose edicts should be followed to the letter. Come on. First off, no one can be that good. If you think you are, such arrogance will in all likelihood prevent you from seeing some basic truths about human behavior, that is to say truths that don't align with your world view. The key to success in UX is to start from a place of humble confidence, not arrogance.

## User experience designers don't design user experiences

UX designers don't design experiences, experiences happen when users encounter a situation and respond to it. They can respond well or badly. All UX designers can do is understand users well enough to design a series of objects, interactions, and/or screens that make sense and work for users—hopefully provoking a positive "experience" in users.

## The most important UX skills are "soft skills"

There's an old saying often attributed to Woody Allen, "90% of life is just showing up." I'd say if you are a UX professional, a good chunk of the remaining 10 percent consists of the soft skills of listening, empathy, and communication. Listen in order to understand the problem and listen to the feedback from users to formulate solutions. Have empathy towards users, so that you can care about what you are doing to help them. Be a good communicator so that you can message your solution and discuss it with the people who have to execute it.

### Simple is hard

In my experience, the best designs are simple designs. Creating simple designs is really hard. Not only do you have to fight your own instinct to make things more complicated than they need to be, you also have to fight that same instinct in everyone you are working with, including stakeholders and product managers. Which is why you need …

### Debate skills

Not only do good UX people have good communication skills, they can also sell their points in the face of critics and cynics who don't like the solutions they've produced.

At the same time, an open "balanced" designer can debate a point but also accept when they are wrong. Because …

### Failing is awesome

In our society failure has a stigma: if you fail then somehow you are a "loser." A huge part of UX design involves conceptual design and user testing, and when we fail (if we are paying attention) we can learn from it. At the very least, when a design we pilot doesn't work we know that particular approach doesn't work. Some of the best insights into people and their behaviors have come from testing designs that users did not understand and/or could not use.

## It's not rocket science

Yes, when you do formal usability testing or user research, there is a certain amount of analysis involved, but it's not that hard. If there were a lot of math involved, frankly, I wouldn't be doing it… because I suck at math.

## Common sense is the best tool a designer has

If a design solution that you or a peer creates doesn't "make sense" then it probably won't make sense to the end users. A big dose of common sense helps designers filter out good ideas from the bad ones. Don't try and "sell" a design that requires leaps in logic and over- thinking things.

## UI design is not that important

I've designed screens and interfaces for over a decade, and what I'm suggesting might make some of my colleagues mad, but I'm going to put it out there: UI design is not that important, and it's not even that hard. It may have been hard ten years ago, but we now have a plethora of design patterns and best practices available for our review and use. We have design guidelines from every major software platform.

Focus (and sweat) the details, yes, but don't try and rethink things that people who are smarter than you have already figured out.

## The best designers know users, not UIs

UI design is not hard. Understanding users and figuring out how to create designs that make their lives better — THAT'S what's hard. The best designers spend their time trying to understand who they are designing for by doing research and interviews. "Know your audience" is a common statement I have heard in multiple domains, and it's absolutely true in UX design as well.

## Usability testing can be done (almost) anywhere

I have built three different usability labs in my career and have done the majority of my usability testing with one laptop in a quiet area (a coffee shop, an empty office). Building out a huge technological terror to do something as simple as testing an initial concept with some users is unnecessary overkill.

## Developers can do UX design, too (and many are really good at it)

I've never been a big fan of "silos" in projects, where a dedicated group of designers do a design and then they hand it over to developers to build it. That's why I like working in an agile team, where developers pitch design ideas just like us UXers do. I've met many developers over the years that could create great useable screens, often better than those the "UX professional" made.

If you are on a team but ignore the talents of many on the team because they aren't "accredited" designers or don't have the right title, well, I pity you. You're missing out on some talent that may be right under your nose.

## Usability is not enough

We have gone beyond usability. Now, UX designers have to think about desirability, about content, and about how to frame the offering to increase usage. Usability is "table stakes."

## We are all storytellers, so tell a good story

Explaining is a huge part of what we do: explaining what we have found out about our users, explaining how we can help users with what we have designed, explaining why a certain feature should be accentuated or de-scoped. The best way to explain is through telling a story, because humans are all storytellers. Some of us are good at it and some of us are not.

The best of us weave a compelling tale, and the best UX professionals know that storytelling is the key to it all.

## Lessons in online reputation protection: Or, think before you post

The Internet has been a huge boon for the world, allowing people from different cultures and countries to communicate and share ideas, providing tools for businesses and users to increase their efficiencies and effectiveness. and it has also given us the perfect medium for us to embarrass ourselves and ruin our careers.

I am referring, of course, to those many instances where people "drunk-blog", or when they - or, in many instances, their friends - post indiscrete information or photos that aren't terribly flattering. Many of this comes from someone saying things like "Hey, watch this!" but more often than not it just resulted in someone not thinking ahead and living (and posting) "in the moment". We all live for the moment to some extent or another, and we often forget that the Internet is public - even Facebook can be exposed to the entire world if your security settings aren't configured to prevent it.

Here's some helpful hints that I have identified that will provide what I call "Online Reputation Protection" insurance. Of course, all coverage is subject to change, depending on any pre-existing conditions you may have.

(Many of these hints are obvious, at least to me, and you may read some of the following and go" Duh!" Well, that's fine - this post is not for you, it's for those poor unfortunate souls who don't think before they act. So, if I can help one person by posting this, then I've done them - and the Internet - a service.)

### The Internet isn't forever - but it's close

Yes, Twitter is not infinitely searchable, and Facebook and Myspace doesn't store everything you post on it. but don't underestimate the power of search engines. Sites like Google cache, well, EVERYTHING. And they have millions of dollars to throw at servers to store those caches for a long long time.

Finally, remember that those social sites you publish on can change their terms and conditions at any time, making what you wrote "just between friends" public to the world at large.

So, when it comes to posting stuff on your favorite social networking site... don't post something you could regret later.

## Potential employers use Google

One of the first things that employers and recruiters do (in addition to the traditional background checks, such as references and credit history) is google your name. If you have no real online activity, you're good to go (though if you've applied for a tech job the employer may wonder why you don't have any online "presence"). If you do have a blog, a twitter account, etc. then they will potentially see everything you have ever posted online, ever. So, like the old saying, don't post something online that you wouldn't want your mother to see (or know) - it may cost you a potential job.

## Politics and religion are very touchy things

Yes, you may be passionate about what you believe in. Absolutely, you can use your website or Twitter account or Facebook to promote your views and causes.

However, remember that in the heat of the moment you may say or do something that might come back and bite you where the sun don't shine. Take this example, for... example. You see a passionate person that posted his political opinion online in the heat of the moment... and he's now, well, screwed. Don't let this happen to you.

Moderate your online opinions - even if you're passionate, don't go nuts. And if you go "all out," don't be surprised if there are repercussions in the real world. because there often is.

## Cursing is allowed. to a point

We all use "salty language" from time to time -
we aren't perfect. But there are still certain words that
our culture finds... well, verboten. One starts with
the letter "n" and the other starts with the letter "c."
Now, in the proper editorial context, one can use both
words with very little consequences - in a quote, for
example, or an etymological study of a word's origin.
Any other situation, though... be careful. Especially
if you are using either word online to refer to an ex-
girlfriend or boyfriend.

## A picture is worth a thousand firings

Don't have to worry about getting a job, because
you already have one? Well, this article is a good
overview of several cases when users posted photos-
or did something online - which resulted in them
losing their jobs. And in this economy, that's not a
good thing - especially when you have to explain
to potential employers why you lost your previous
position. "

On several instances a photo that someone has
posted has resulted in someone being fired- especially
if the photo showed that the person who "called in
sick" was actually at a Halloween party - like in this
instance.

(A quick sidebar - Halloween is an especially
dangerous time of year when it comes to potential
impacts to your online reputation. Copious alcohol
plus skimpy costumes, add in a dash of camera

phones and ubiquitous internet access... well, you can see what can happen.)

You also have to worry about old photos of you that other people post online, from years back. Photos that can make you look like a real dweeb.

## We don't have editors - and we all need them

What I find so interesting about the Internet is it give users the opportunity to throw out a thought or a video almost instantly. And because the number of steps between the thought and the publication of the thought is so low, we just throw our thoughts out there... without thinking. And sometimes, there is no "undo."

In the heat of the moment so many people forget that expression and information is available to anyone who uses a browser and has an Internet connection. We don't have editors, so dedicate a part of your mind to help you focus on "self-editing."

The life... and career... that you save, may be your own.

# The Rise of Enablers

I travel quite a bit for work, and as I recently sat in a hotel room, I started thinking about all the steps that brought me to that room. I booked the flight and the room online; I flew from Atlanta to Boston and I took a cab to the hotel... A typical business trip, with no problems or delays. Breaking things down, I started counting off all the technological innovations that supported me in that journey... "enablers" that made things happen and made things easy. Here's just a few of them:

- I was able to compare flights online, both times and flights

- I was able to compare hotels online, both price and location

- I checked traffic before I drove to the airport on my GPS.

- I used to GPS to get directions to the airport (that routed me around traffic)

- I checked in to my flight through the Delta app on my iPhone

- I changed my seat using that same app

- I was able to track my checked bag using the app

- I was able to use an electronic boarding pass to go through security

- I read news articles and watched videos on my iPad in the airport, using free Internet access

- I was able to write a status report for work on my iPad that automatically synced to my laptop via the cloud

- I confirmed the address of my hotel through the Marriott app

- I paid for my taxi ride with a credit card using a card reader that was mounted in the taxi

And if I spent more time pondering, I'm sure I could easily double this list.

Because we use them every day, we tend to forget is just how amazing these advances are. If you are old enough, think back to a time when you may have taken a similar trip, maybe ten or twenty years ago. You had none of the above to help you on your way, everything took longer

and things were more complicated. You had to spend time with a travel agent, you had to have sufficient cash to pay the taxi, you would have gotten stuck in traffic because you had no way of knowing there was a wreck backing up cars for miles... It was, well, kinda hard.

To make a direct point, what is happening throughout society is that technology is streamlining processes and helping people do things faster and easier than ever before. These enablers are becoming omnipresent and ubiquitous. They are also impacting society in negative ways... For example, the aforementioned travel agent is becoming an endangered species, and that isn't the only job category that has been impacted by these enablers.

What is even more exciting to me than seeing how far technology has helped us every day is that companies are still actively coming up with new enablers. One of the big stories in technology this week is a computer peripheral called the Leap, a small box the size of a pack of chewing gum that offers gesture recognition far superior to the (previously groundbreaking) Kinect Xbox controller. The promise of gesture-based computing, as predicted in Minority Report, is one step closer to reality, and as a designer the possibilities that brings excites me.

We often think of the "old days," and whimsically say to ourselves "things were simpler then." I'd like to counter

that statement, as in many ways' things are simpler NOW. We just have so many enablers to choose from, things look more complicated than they actually are. Ask the typical man on the street if they would like to go back to getting their food, the way people used to in "the good old days"... by growing it themselves... and see if you'll see them pining for that nostalgic past after that.

# Usability for Evil: Six Flags Meal Deals

One of my new favorite sites is Usability for Evil, which shows examples of web sites that benefits the companies behind the sites far more than the users of said sites.

Well, I had a personal experience with such a site this week and I got to share it with you

The site is the one for Six Flags Theme Parks, which I went to so I could pre-order tickets for my family to go the local Atlanta park. At the site they also sell meal and snack vouchers, and if you go here you can see quite a lot of really helpful information that tells you that you can "save time and money" by prepaying for your food. It also implies, by the verbiage and repeated use of the words "online meal deal," that you won't be able to get these "deals" at the parks.

My wife suggested I buy some vouchers ahead

of time (she, like I, assumed they would save us "time and money"). So, I did, one voucher for three refillable drink cups, three vouchers for refillable cotton candy (or popcorn) buckets, and two for funnel cakes.

The vouchers used the same web-based software that the tickets used, and it took several minutes to print them all - one voucher per sheet. "Save time and money?" I guess that didn't include the cost of the ink I used to print them.

We arrived and I quickly discovered something that started my day of "fun" off on the wrong foot. The price of the items I pre-purchased were EXACTLY THE SAME at the parks. So much for "saving money." So much for not being intentionally misled. How about time? Surely, I'd save that, right?

The first vendor I went to with my voucher for the drink cups said that I couldn't use that at his station (even though his food booth had a sticker saying that it did). I'd have to go to a nearby restaurant, because that particular voucher could only be used at one of the restaurants (and this was on the voucher - in small type).

So, I went to the restaurant, got the cups, and then later I tried to get the cotton candy buckets.

"Oh, I don't have any cotton candy buckets. Only popcorn."

I saw over her shoulder, hanging on the wall, bags of bucket-sized cotton candy. Next to popcorn buckets.

"Can't you just empty one of the popcorn buckets and put cotton candy in it?"

"Oh, I can't do that." Sigh.

After the third vendor that either A) would not take my vouchers or B) did not know HOW to take my vouchers or C) did not sell the food I was trying to by, I realized the error of my ways.

I had exchanged real currency for fake currency, buying color printouts that were only good at certain places in a theme park. As opposed to the elegant and simple way the Disney Dining Plan works (it's on your hotel key, and uses a simple point system), the process of exchanging these vouchers was a byzantine nightmare that was certainly not "fun."

They made buying food an exercise in bureaucracy.

When all was said and done, I was finally able to "claim" all the food I had pre-purchased, but my mood was darkened by a cloud of frustration and anger at incompetent service. How many times have people like me been "suckered" into buying these meal vouchers and then "give up", never getting the food they pre-paid for?

When will my next trip to Six Flags be? Oh, how about never?

(I've found in my research over the years that positive experiences are quickly forgotten, and negative experiences linger - like this one).

In closing, instead of taking this as a warning to not buy Six Flags food vouchers, take this lesson to heart if you are a user experience professional. Designing an affective web form or site for a company is not enough if the total user experience the company provides well, stinks.

Instead of enjoying my day, I played "claim your food" and the experience was a pretty terrible one. This is one of the reasons I go back to Disney time and again - I almost never have a bad experience at one of their parks like I did in this example and their staff (gasp!) actually know what they are doing.

Six Flags, good luck. You'll need it.

## The baseline is shifting

I had a great meeting with my team this week discussing customer expectations and needs. As part of the discussion the Kano model, which I was only slightly familiar with, came up. Created in the 1980s, the Kano model explores how customers perceive aspects/features of a product or service. These features can be perceived as "hygiene" (a feature has to and is expected to be there) to "delighters" (features that WOW customers) and as a company you want to provide as many "delighters" as possible.

What got me intrigued when about this model is that a core aspect of the idea is that, over time, customer's expectations shift. What was once "delighters" become expected, and the baseline shifts. The challenge is if you are creating a product that will be delivered a year from now, you have to target the "new baseline" (which is exactly what I am facing on my project).

The idea that the baseline is shifting is exactly right and is a real challenge that businesses are facing. What was acceptable practice and offerings five years ago just isn't

anymore, and some businesses will have to adjust to the new baseline or fail.

Let's look at how the baseline has shifted, in some obvious ways:

### The stock market

Want to buy or sell stocks? Fifteen years ago, you would have had to have a broking account or a dedicated broker who you would call to buy shares. Or your accountant would do it for you. Now? Well, I just bought more Apple stock on my computer about five minutes ago, without any of the friction that the previous process had. I can also do the same thing on my mobile phone. Which brings me to:

### Mobile phones

Again, just a few years ago the idea that I could compose e-mail, browse web pages, or play high-resolution games on my phone would have been considered science fiction. Now, thanks to Apple, Google, RIM and many other companies, this is now the new norm.

### Home-video editing

Need to edit a video? The first video editing setup I had was an Amiga, with a very expensive hardware add- on card called the Video Toaster (and yes, I am that old).

It brought me the ability to do video production and editing in ways that were previously reserved to television stations. Now I can edit video at a higher resolution much quicker on my iPad, a piece of hardware thinner than the majority of magazines you can buy.

Now let's look at how the baseline is shifting today:

## Magazines (and the publishing industry)

Jann Wenner, the publisher of Rolling Stone, recently stated in an interview that magazines will be around for "decades." The fact that he was so confident and certain of that fact well, let me just state that the baseline is shifting dramatically in the publishing industry, and some people aren't quite ready to adjust to a new quickly- coming reality. Customers are consuming content differently, and paper for many is no longer the preferred medium.

## The service industry

Customers' expectations are increasing, and companies that do not service these new expectations will lose customers and money. The Zappos company understands this, and continuously focus on providing delightful experiences to their customers. Apple, with the hands-on support it provides with its Apple stores, acknowledge this new reality. Companies that don't accept and embrace the new baseline face tough times in an even tougher economy.

### The entertainment industry.

Customers have lot of choices in the way they consume their entertainment, and the smart companies are embracing the new digital mediums. Blockbuster Video was stuck in the old delivery mechanism of physical media, and they are all but defunct against the cheap streaming offering Netflix provides.

So, the main thing to take away is simply this: Understand, as much as you can, how people think today but plan for that thinking to change.

A final thought: I went to a book sale a while back and saw the book "The End of Marketing As we Know it" Sergio Zyman. It was incredibly popular at the time of publication (1999), but now? It was selling for $1, and nobody was buying it. What happened? The ideas that was in that book was based on the old baseline, and, at the time, were perceived as forward-thinking and revolutionary. Now? Old ideas old news. Again, the baseline had shifted.

## Don't design with "something to prove"

I'm wrapping up a long-term design project, and, after two years working on the same thing, I've learned a lot. A lot about myself, a lot about design, and a lot about people.

One of the things that I notice over this time was that different designers on my team took design criticism differently. Some of them would be completely open to feedback and respond collaboratively. Others… well, it was worse than saying that their children were ugly – they acted as if you were trying to actually KILL their children. They responded loudly… and sometimes aggressively. Any criticism you provided was unfounded, and you were stupid to provide it.

That's the response I got when I dared suggest another way of thinking of the design. And these were people who, in the structure of the project, worked for me.

For a while, I thought it was a reflection of these people's maturity and experience. Nope, that wasn't it. Some junior designers were a lot more professional in dealing with criticism that the senior ones. Maybe that was it… Maybe the senior people felt that they were above criticism. But no, that didn't explain it (not fully at least).

I think I finally figured it out. The key was a conversation that I had with one of my designers about a design I had done late last year. Because of some aggressive deadlines, I had to take over a feature that needed someone with my reputation of "getting things done" to come in and finish it. I did my work – quickly – and then went on vacation for the Christmas holidays.

I returned to see that work had, of course, continued to take place in my absence. The designer had inherited my work and had changed some things I had done. Here's the thing: I'm never precious about anything I do, creatively or professionally. Some of my best work has been done when I had someone who I could collaborate with, and that someone often made good work better because they cast a critical eye upon it. So, my initial response was "let's see what he did," not "how dare he change what I did!"

We did a design walkthrough, and, sure enough, the good design I had done was made better. Extra steps and options that distracted the user from the core task were removed. It was now something that was easier to learn and use. I thanked my colleague and complimented him on the good work… and that is when I realized why some designers couldn't take criticism well.

They lacked confidence in what they did. In every instance over the past two years, I could look back at why the designer was defensive… and it was because he or she were insecure. Not just in the designs they did, but they lacked confidence in themselves. They could not separate themselves from the work because they're sense of self was wrapped up in what they had done. They weren't designing to solve problems, or focused on the users, and instead they were trying to prove themselves… TO themselves.

This is not criticism of them, personally… we all have our faults (mine's in California). But as I have written before, the work is a reflection of us… it's not who we are. We need to have a healthy separation. Be passionate, absolutely… but don't lose the proper perspective. That way, when the work is done and responded to (and often criticized) we can react to what people say appropriately, and professionally.

## The future is not what it used to be

Time is broken.

Well, it may not be broken, but, from where I stand, it isn't moving at the same pace it used to. Maybe it's because I'm about to cross a particularly notable threshold (I leave my 30s in four days) or maybe... it's because time is speeding up.

I'm not talking about anything like information overload, a clear and present danger in our plugged-in age. I'm talking about the future - the event horizon that is supposed to be always beyond our grasp. It's here. It's arrived, and it's not what it used to be.

Let me explain. One of my favorite shows is Mad Men, a show set in the early 1960s, and the touches of technology they showcase in their episodes are usually perceived as amazing marvels that all the characters get excited about. The first season episode where the office gets a Xerox machine is particularly memorable- the secretaries linger around it like groupies (BTW, the machine also has a Twitter account).

Today... well, we are surrounded by marvels, and no one notices. As Louie CK so famously said on the Conan O'Brien show "Everything is amazing, and no one is happy." The constant exposure to technology has cheapened it - it is now commonplace, something taken for granted. and when (to quote that great ad slogan for the classic movie Westworld) "something goes worng", people go crazy. Both Google's Gmail and Twitter suffered prolonged outages the past month, and people reacted like someone shot their new puppy.

(Let's hope no one every sets off an EMP over the west coast... because we will have a LOT more problems to deal with than Twitter being down...)

The Future of Today is really great in many ways... but It's not Star Trek's utopia, nor it's Blade Runner's dystopia, it's... today. Now.

The Future of Today.

Remember the future we dreamed about as a kid? With jet packs and rocket cars and tickets to the moon? Well, the pace of innovation has brought us that future, but instead of technology bringing all of us out to new frontiers, it has helped us work from home- from our bed, even. It has helped us keep in touch with friends and relatives we would never talk to on a regular basis without it - artificial relationships, courtesy of Facebook and Myspace. It has drawn us inward, not outward.

So, if you have read this so far, you are probably going, "what in frak does this have to do with user experience design?" (Well, you may not use the word "frak," unless you are a Battlestar Galactica fan)

Well, everything.

Technology is the reason we all HAVE jobs designing applications and researching users. It has also produced behavioral and attitudinal changes that will have impacts on our society for decades. We need to appreciate the future we have been given and be keenly aware of how technology is changing how people work, live, and thrive.

The best example, to me, is in the mobile space. Can you imagine living without your mobile device, even if it is only a "dumb" phone, free with contract? Yeah, me neither. The ubiquitous access to technology through mobile devices is changing where people do things and how people do things. If you are UX designer or researcher and am not paying attention to this - you better start. Otherwise, like the typesetters of the previous century, you may quickly find yourself out of a job.

Attitudes, too, are changing. There is something I call the Immediacy of Now- the growing desire to know or do something immediately. The mobile devices are a part of it, but there is also the patience levels of users. I have noticed it has been decreasing over time, and this, again, is a reflection of how technology has reset expectations. Pay this close attention.

Finally, there is the expectations that systems are smarter that they usually are. With all the new Web 2.0 apps and sites that users have been exposed to over the past few years, their baseline has been raised. Gen Y, especially, have high expectations when it comes to what a web service or product should provide. Be prepared to raise the bar to meet those expectations.

In the Future of Today, impatience is a virtue. Time... and the future, waits for no one.

Experience (Still) Matters

## About Joseph Dickerson

Joseph Dickerson is a User Experience professional focused on designing innovative on-line and mobile applications. With a decade of experience in software design and user research, Dickerson has made it his mission to make technology easier for people to use.

He has led ethnographic research efforts on a variety of topics (from mobile usage to Gen Y to personal payments and small businesses), as well as provided usability and design services for many different companies.

Joseph writes on design and other topics at http:// www.josephdickerson.com

www.ingramcontent.com/pod-product-compliance
Lightning Source LLC
LaVergne TN
LVHW051331050326
832903LV00031B/3476